Consumer Behaviour

A Practical Guide

Gordon R. Foxall

London and New York

First published in 1980 by Croom Helm Ltd
Reprinted 1982, 1984, 1985 and 1986

Reprinted 1988, 1991 by Routledge
11 New Fetter Lane, London EC4P 4EE

Published in the USA by
Routledge
in association with Routledge, Chapman & Hall, Inc.
29 West 35th Street, New York NY 10001

Printed and bound in Great Britain by
Biddles Ltd, Guildford and King's Lynn

British Library Cataloguing in Publication Data

Foxall, Gordon R.
    Consumer Behaviour — Revised ed.
    1. Consumers
    I. Title
    658.8′34   HF5415.2

    ISBN 0-415-00892-1 Pbk

Library of Congress Cataloging in Publication Data

ISBN 0-415-00892-1 (Pbk)

CONTENTS

TABLES

FIGURES

TO JEAN

PREFACE

Consumer behaviour is a rapidly expanding field of research and teaching which, as well as being intellectually stimulating for the academic researcher, is of considerable value to marketing managers and others who are professionally concerned with buying activity. This book is intended to reflect the current status of the consumer behaviour field and its readers should include both managers and students of marketing, business management and the social sciences. Growing interest in the consumer on the part of behavioural scientists, geographers, planners and home economists makes the book suitable for students and practitioners in a wide range of professions.

Not all behavioural science concepts are equally appropriate for the study of marketing and the emphasis in these chapters is on the critical evaluation of those concepts which have actually been found useful in the analysis and prediction of consumer behaviour. Sometimes writers have expressed great faith in certain sociological and social psychological notions which, in practice, have little to contribute to more effective decision making. While some of these concepts have a place in any account of consumer behaviour because they still appear to be potentially useful, and are thus included in this book, they have not been accorded the space and consideration which has been given to concepts and techniques which have already proved relevant to marketing management. Limitations of space and a desire that this should be a practical volume have made such a course inevitable. Similarly, diagrams and tables have not been multiplied unnecessarily and are provided only where they are worth while in illustrating research findings.

After an introductory chapter which contains an account of behavioural science in marketing and the buying process, the book first analyses the behaviour of individual customers. In doing so, it draws on such concepts as perception, learning, personality and attitudes. The behaviour of aggregates of consumers is next explained. Useful concepts in this endeavour are reference groups, the family, culture and social class. The concluding chapter is concerned with the integration and application of behavioural concepts to marketing decision making and examines models of consumer behaviour, consumer loyalty, and the claim that marketing and advertising manipulate consumers.

ACKNOWLEDGEMENTS

The author wishes to thank the publishers of *The Advertising Quarterly* and *The Quarterly Review of Marketing* for permission to reproduce material previously printed in those journals.

PART I : INTRODUCTION

1 MARKETING AND THE CONSUMER

Modern marketing thought stresses the need of business managers to know who their customers are and why they choose their products rather than those of rival firms. Marketing is not a case of finding or inducing someone to buy whatever the firm happens to manufacture. Nowadays successful management depends more than ever on matching every aspect of the business product, advertising, after-sales service and so on to the satisfaction of consumer needs. This is the essence of consumer-orientation as an integrated approach to business management.

Consumer-orientation stems from the firm's adoption and implementation of the Marketing Concept, a philosophy of business organisation which has three major implications: firstly, the success of any firm depends above all on the consumer and what he or she is willing to accept and pay for; secondly, the firm must be aware of what the market wants well before production commences, and, in the case of highly technological industries, long before production is even planned; and thirdly, consumer wants must be continually monitored and measured so that, through product and market development, the firm keeps ahead of its competitors.

Obviously, this concept of business management is not founded on altruism. It emphasises the profitability of the firm as well as the satisfaction of buyers by showing that profits follow service. The following statement of the marketing concept illustrates these points:

The marketing message is that the consumers........are the arbiters of fortune in business, and rightly so; and that by consulting the interest of the consumers systematically both before production is undertaken and throughout the process of distribution, industrial and commercial activity not only brings forth wanted goods and services in a timely and thus economical and profitable manner, but also reveals itself in its proper role, thriving in its service to the community, raising the standard of living and meriting the reward it receives. [1]

In a competitive economic system, therefore, the survival and growth of firms requires accurate knowledge about consumers: how they buy, why they buy and where they buy as well as just what they buy. Critics of marketing contend that this is unnecessary, that it is possible to manipulate hapless buyers into parting with their money in return for products they do not want. The reality of marketing was stated recently by a director of Unilever, Lord Trenchard,[2] in terms which show such criticism to be ill founded:

> The concept that technology can decide what the consumer shall have, and the advertiser can condition her to want, is laughable. Every new activity in the food market starts with finding out what consumers want. Many of the largest companies have learnt from experience that if they get it wrong no amount of advertising on earth will compensate. Seventy per cent of new food products fail.

It is not surprising, then, that considerable interest has been expressed in using the behavioural sciences, especially social psychology and sociology, to understand the consumer. As a result, consumers' psychological backgrounds have been investigated in order to establish the extent to which factors like attitudes, motives and personality traits affect buying behaviour; and social influences such as class, status and the family have also been examined for their contribution to our understanding of consumer decision making. The following chapters are concerned with concepts and variables such as these and their usefulness in consumer research. Before this is done, however, it will be valuable to look at recent trends in the application of behavioural science to marketing in order to appreciate the necessity of a critical approach to the study of consumer behaviour.

Behavioural Science

Whatever differences of opinion separate the various types of social scientist, all are agreed on the complexity of their subject matter. None disputes that human behaviour is influenced by a multiplicity of interacting forces and that it presents a very considerable challenge to anyone who attempts to unravel the motivating factors that shape it.

Consumer behaviour contains a particular difficulty in that, superficially at least, it gives the impression that it ought to be relatively easy to understand and explain, even to predict. Basic economics assures us that the quantity of a good demanded is inversely related to price, and even a cursory reflection on the importance of money in industrial societies suggests that economics is right. Of course, economists are quick to point out that there are many real-world deviations from such a rudimentary theory; and familiarity with the actual behaviour of consumers is apt to focus the researcher's attention almost entirely on these deviations rather than on what theory predicts.

Generally, the more consumer researchers have appreciated the complexity of customers' behaviour, the more they have tended to look beyond formal economics for explanations of such activity. Whereas less than twenty years ago a reviewer of household buying behaviour [3] emphasised the influence of income as the major determinant of purchase choices, it is usual nowadays for consumer researchers to explain such decision making in terms of a wide range of stimuli and response mechanisms. However, some economists have developed alternative approaches to the study of consumer behaviour such as the 'behavioural economics' associated with George Katona. [4] Katona's work concerns the effects of consumers' expectations on aggregate levels of demand, business and consumer motivations to spend, save and invest, and consumer attitudes in times of inflation and deflation.

The application of behavioural science to marketing has not, however, proceeded smoothly. It has tended to be lopsided, confused and uncritical, all of which have tended to reduce its efficacy both in academic or educational terms and in making a practical contribution to marketing. Too much reliance has been placed on psychology and insufficient attention given to other disciplines, particularly sociology but also geography and anthropology.

That psychology, particularly social psychology, has made important contributions to our understanding of consumer behaviour cannot be disputed, of course, and in a recent review, Ramond [5] lists the following concepts and techniques from psychology which have been widely incorporated into marketing studies: perception including absolute threshold; just noticeable difference and perceptual defence; cognitive dissonance; learning including reinforcement; stochastic models; traits (psychographics). The list could be extended, at least to include attitudes and motivation, and although it will be argued in later chapters that some of these concepts have had only a very limited impact on marketing, it is significant that there are so many of them. All that the reviewer came up with from sociology was the single notion of social class, and he comments that 'if social class weren't such an important variable, the tautologies and truisms of sociology would be easier to deride'.

In view of the psychologists' claims that their discipline is *the* study of behaviour, it is, perhaps, not surprising that so much attention has been given to the psychology of the consumer. Indeed, behavioural scientists in marketing have displayed great zeal in trying to depict consumer behaviour simply as a function of what occurs in the consumer's psyche, his 'black box' or 'central control unit'. Indeed, so great is this emphasis, that there has been little room, even in so called comprehensive models of consumer buying processes, for the influence of social structure on people's choice of goods and services.

Consumer behaviour is a confused field of study because consumer researchers in universities and polytechnics, to whom falls the problem of establishing an integrated discipline, suffer from role ambiguity. Are they primarily academic researchers or should they be pursuing managerial objectives? These need not be mutually exclusive, of course, but there is a tendency to regard them as difficult to reconcile. Neither academic progress nor marketing practice seem to have come off too well from this uncertainty. Marketing academics have often engaged in consultancy and contract work for retailing and industrial firms; but, despite such co-operation, it is not unusual to find areas where there still exists a large amount of mutual suspicion and a feeling that most things academic are of little, if any, practical value.

This also means that much consumer research has been undertaken on an *ad hoc* basis with little regard for theory or even the integration of new empirical results into the present body of factual knowledge. Several years ago, Philip Kotler [6] wrote that 'the contemporary effort of behavioural scientists in marketing is to analyse well specific aspects of behaviour in the hope that someday someone will put them all together' but there are still few signs that this synthesis is taking place and the situation seems only to have increased in complexity and confusion since then.

A further criticism of the study of consumer behaviour stems from the refusal of some researchers and writers to evaluate the relevance of the concepts, variables and methods which they have 'borrowed' from the parent disciplines. A well-known consumer behaviour textbook [7] opens with an account of several social scientists discussing why a consumer bought a particular car. The imaginary learned assembly consists of an economist, a sociologist, an anthropologist and *two* psychologists. It is not at all surprising when each of the psychologists offers his own unique explanation of the purchase they have just witnessed, or when the sociologist and the anthropologist cannot decide which aspects of the sale each of them is qualified to explain.

It is usual in texts on consumer behaviour to see each variable or each school of thought within a discipline presented separately and accompanied by an account of the implications of each one for marketing practice. This uncritical approach gives the impression that all the variables or schools of thought are of equal importance both in the study of consumer behaviour and in the parent disciplines themselves. In fact, some approaches are diametrically opposed to others; to accept one is to reject the rest. It is thus misleading to present them side by side as though marketing could simply take what it requires from each school and forget the remainder. The meanings attached to key concepts differ from one school to another and this can only mean confusion if consumer researchers fail to distinguish between them. While it is clearly not the job of the consumer researcher to become involved in the internal disputes of the parent disciplines, once ideas and techniques are transferred to a new context, they must surely be scrutinised for their suitability and validity.

There remains a great deal of controversy in psychology, sociology, anthropology and other behavioural sciences, as well as between these disciplines, about the explanation of human behaviour. Marketing need not become embroiled in this controversy but care must be taken to ensure that explanations of consumer behaviour are consistent and rigorous, and that the behavioural assumptions underlying particular explanations are explicit.

This book concentrates on the use of social psychology and sociology to elucidate the behaviour of consumers (see Figure 1.1).

Figure 1.1 : Social and Individual Factors in Consumer Choice

Aspects of the Social Structure	Individual Influences
Reference Groups	Personality (traits and types)
The Family	Self concepts
Social Class	Attitudes
Culture	Perception and learning
etc.	Dissonance etc.

CONSUMER DECISION MAKING

Attempts are often made to distinguish these disciplines from one another and this is usually done in terms of their differing levels of analysis or viewpoints since their subject matters are substantially the same. Social psychologists are said to be interested primarily in individuals and their concern with group behaviour is preoccupied with the effects of social behaviour on the individual's attitudes and personality. Sociologists are normally depicted as being interested above all in the structure and functioning of groups and their relationship to social institutions such as the family, education, industry, class and culture. In reality, the differences that once divided behavioural scientists are becoming blurred as social psychologists are increasingly taking aspects of the social structure into consideration while sociologists are becoming more and more interested in the actions of individuals. Some division of labour is still to be found but in jointly executed work it is often difficult to unravel the elements contributed by the social psychologist from those of the sociologist.

In an eclectic and generally empirical discipline like marketing it is therefore unnecessary to make too sharp a distinction between these subjects. Rather, it seems reasonable to assume that consumer behaviour can develop as a single behavioural science. Certainly this is preferable to the development of consumer psychology and consumer sociology as separate and competitive fields, since that would only preserve an artificial dichotomy and would not add to our knowledge of the interplay of a variety of factors which influences the behaviour of individuals and groups.

Above all consumer behaviour is likely to develop best if it remains a practical subject, involved in marketing decision making as well as academic research. Too often in the past there has been a communications gap between academic consumer behaviour specialists and marketing practitioners. This is a consequence of disagreements among social scientists about the meanings of concepts and their application, from the fact that research can easily become preoccupied with theoretical topics, and from misunderstandings about the needs of businessmen.[8] As was stated above, the present situation is one in which neither the aims of the businessman nor those of the marketing scientist are likely to be fulfilled. The following criteria [9] are intended to ensure that the continued application of behavioural science to marketing advances the objectives of both these groups. They do not constitute a checklist which can be routinely applied at the end of a piece of research; they are general principles which should be borne in mind by researchers at all stages of their work.

1. Does this concept or technique explain an aspect of marketing behaviour which was hitherto fully or partially unexplained?
2. Does the concept or technique have implications for marketing planning, policies or strategies?
3. Does this concept or technique relate aspects of the wider social

structure to the individual's socio-psychological make-up and thus help determine his consumption choices?

Hopefully the inclusion of such questions in our frame of reference will help avoid partial, confused or uncritical approaches to further investigation of the consumer.

However valuable introspection on the part of social and consumer researchers may be, it is not the primary intention of this book to deal with the discipline of consumer behaviour in its own right. Rather, the focus of attention is on increasing the understanding of consumer behaviour among marketing managers and other businessmen.

Models of Consumer Behaviour

Many fundamental facts about consumer behaviour can, of course, be obtained quite easily. For example, we know that about eighty per cent of shopping trips begin and end at home; that more than half are made on foot and nearly a quarter by bus; that most of the remainder involve car travel.

Data such as these are often useful for planners, transport managers and retailers. But description of consumer movements is normally insufficient on its own for many of the other agencies concerned with the consumer. Government organisations set up to educate or protect the customer need information about the social, psychological and business forces that influence purchasing. Home economists often find that knowledge about consumer choices is basic to their work. And business managers themselves are vitally and centrally concerned with the wants, needs and aspirations of their firms' customers.

The complexity inherent in understanding consumer behaviour has led some researchers to construct models of the buying process which indicate the stages through which the consumer passes from the time he or she first becomes aware of a need for a product or service to the time when a product has been purchased, a brand selected, and the consumer is evaluating the success of his purchase and deciding whether he will buy that particular product and/or brand again. At the same time, such models usually indicate the social and psychological forces which shape the potential buyer's actions at each stage in the process.

The more comprehensive models of the buying process are useful in specifying possible relationships between variables and in suggesting hypotheses which may be empirically tested. Most of those which have been put forward [10] are elaborate computer flow diagrams which show the stages in the consumer's decision process and the behavioural inputs which can be used to explain his actions. More will be said about these models and the advantages and disadvantages which stem from their use, in a later chapter.

Less elaborate mathematical models have been considered by Kotler [11]   and a 'marketing continuum model' has been proposed by Jenkins. [12]   The latter portrays the consumer as moving from a state of unawareness through phases of awareness, comprehension, conviction, preference, intent-to-buy and purchase-evaluation to the point at which he considers the repurchase of his selected brand. Models of human behaviour advanced by social scientists not primarily concerned with man the consumer have also been examined for their applicability to marketing. [13]   Thus there is the Marshallian model, the Freudian model, the Veblenian model and the Hobbesian model, all of which have thrown some light on the behaviour of consumers and some of which are mentioned further in later chapters.

Despite the sophistication which has been achieved in the building of consumer behaviour models, and their usefulness in academic research, it is probably fair to say that the majority of models mean little to the businessman who requires a general understanding of how his customers act and react rather than the type of framework which is necessary for the execution of a full-blown scientific research project.[14]   It is valuable, nevertheless, to be able to organise what we learn about the consumer and so the following account of the most obvious features of the buying process may be profitably borne in mind as a context for the concepts and variables which will be introduced in the chapters that follow.

The Buying Process

Consumption is a process which begins well before a product is purchased and which extends well beyond it. Four distinct stages can be recognised:

1. the development and perception of a want or need;
2. pre-purchase planning and decision making;
3. the purchase act itself; and
4. post-purchase behaviour which may lead to repeat buying, repeat sales.

Like more elaborate models this description simplifies and abstracts from reality; some artificiality is inevitable in all attempts to generalise about human behaviour. But it allows the student of consumer behaviour the opportunity to isolate some of the social, psychological and business influences on consumer choice without unduly complicating the process. Its value will be seen as we follow a hypothetical consumer through the various stages involved in purchasing behaviour (see Figure 1.2)

Figure 1.2 : The Buying Process—A Basic Representation

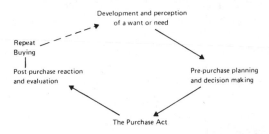

Some writers refer to the first stage as that of the 'growing consciousness of a need' the potential customer becomes aware of a want which can be satisfied through the marketing system. There is always opportunity for firms to innovate by developing products which satisfy needs for which there is currently no adequate market offering but complete innovation is rare. More common is the stimulation of already existing wants through advertising and sales promotion, the creation as it were of a latent demand. Even so-called impulse-buying requires some kind of stimulus.

Having grown aware of a want, the consumer looks for something which may satisfy it. This involves an appraisal of the products and brands on offer and available in the market-place. Consumers are, of course, not as economically rational as basic economics would have us believe, and their knowledge of the market is usually limited; they may easily be misinformed about what is available, its price, its reputation, and so on. The informative and persuasive functions of advertising are thus of immense importance at this stage too, but so are interpersonal influences. It may be that the desire for the product originated through the consumer's contact with another person; it is almost certain that, in the case of a fairly expensive, infrequently bought item, he will seek information from friends, neighbours or relatives about the relative merits of different brands. Indeed, several studies indicate that informal, word-of-mouth communication may be much more effective than formal advertising in moulding consumers' decisions.

Decisions about brand choice continue right up to the moment of purchase; even if the consumer is fairly certain of a brand before he goes to the shop, there is the possibility of his being influenced by point-of-sale advertising or by the salesman. Furthermore, the purchase act does not consists of a single decision, that of brand choice. It is a complex selection involving sub-decisions regarding time and place of purchase, the possibility of mail order buying rather than a store purchase, and the method of payment, e.g., cash sale or hire purchase.

The marketing manager's interest in consumer buying does not end when a purchase has been made. Firms that survive do so because they create loyalty in their customers, because they develop groups of customers who buy the same brand again and again or who frequently patronise the same shop. In order for this to occur customers clearly must be satisfied with their purchases. The company must do all within its power to make sure that its buyers are pleased with what they buy even to the extent of reassuring them after their purchase that they have have chosen the right brand.

Naturally, the consumer who becomes aware of a need may not follow all these procedures and make a purchase: lack of funds or conflicting interests may cause him to give his attention to some other activity. But, if he does go through the stages of the buying process described here, it is certain that his precise behaviour will be modified and shaped by his attitudes, his self-concept, his general motivation and personality, and often by his social class, his stage in the family life cycle and the groups to which he belongs. Unravelling the nature of these influences on the consumer's choice is the basic task of behavioural science in marketing.

Notes

1.   J.D. Straton-Ferrier, 'Marketing: the concept, the function and the man', in *Careers in Marketing*, Pan, 1968, p. 9.

2.   *Guardian*, 4 May 1976.

3.   R. Ferber, 'Research on household behaviour', *American Economic Review*, 52, 1962, p. 19.

4.   See, *inter alia*, G. Katona, 'Psychology and consumer economics', *Journal of Consumer Research*, 1, 1, 1974.

5.   C. Ramond, *The Art of Using Science in Marketing*, Harper and Row, 1974, Chapter 5.

6.   P. Kotler, 'Mathematical models of individual buyer behaviour', *Behavioural Science*, 13, 1968.

7.   J.F. Engel, D.T. Kollat and R.D. Blackwell, *Consumer Behaviour*, Holt, 1968.

8.   J.R.G. Jenkins, *Marketing and Customer Behaviour*, Pergamon, 1972.

9. G.R. Foxall, 'Aspects of the application of behavioural science to marketing', *European Journal of Marketing*, 8, 3, 1974.

10. See, for instance, F.M. Nicosia, *Consumer Decision Processes*, Prentice-Hall, 1966; J.A. Howard and J.N. Sheth, *A Theory of Buyer Behaviour*, Wiley, 1969.

11. Kotler, 'Mathematical models of individual buyer behaviour'.

12. Jenkins, *Marketing and Customer Behaviour*.

13. P. Kotler, 'Behavioural models for analysing buyers', *Journal of Marketing*, 29, 1965.

14. J. Jacoby, 'Consumer research: a state of the art review', *Journal of Marketing*, 42, 1978.

PART II : INDIVIDUAL CONSUMER BEHAVIOUR

2 PERCEPTION AND LEARNING

Products and services are not usually purchased simply for their functional values but also, sometimes primarily, for the social and psychological meanings they convey. For example, cars are seldom chosen for transportation purposes value alone but because they confer status or prestige on their owners. A glance at people's modes of dress indicates that clothes are not desired simply to hide nakedness or confer warmth and protection. Style, colour and quality reflect the wearer's status, associations, self-image and attitudes, as well as his more obvious characteristics like age and social class. Thus the marketing manager needs to be aware of the perceptions his customers and potential customers have of themselves, their social worlds and the products available to them. As a result of this need, our first examination of the behavioural sciences in marketing concerns cognition: the activity involved in thinking, reflecting and understanding.

What Is Perception?

As with so many of the terms encountered in the behavioural sciences, *perception* is used rather vaguely in everyday discourse but must be understood more precisely if it is to be useful in explaining aspects of human behaviour. This does not mean that we have to construct a definition of great scientific weight in order to appreciate its relevance to the study of consumer behaviour, however. Consider the following interpretations.

Engel *et al* [1] understand perception to mean 'the process whereby stimuli are received and interpreted by the individual and translated into a response', while Walters [2] refers to it as 'the entire process by which an individual becomes aware of his environment and interprets it so that it will fit into his own frame of reference'. Both of these statements will be particularly helpful when we discuss the importance of perception for marketing management.

Two facets of perception are of especial interest. First, people become aware of their environment through the five senses and therefore *sensation* is the process with which perception begins. But perception is not synonymous with sensation, despite their clear inter-connectedness. It is true that some writers have presented perception basically in terms of the five senses, as does the following paradigm put forward by Young: [3]

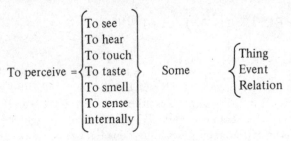

Equally important, and this is the second facet, is the process of interpretation which depends on the socio-psychological meanings the individual attaches to the object perceived (the stimulus). Perceptions of reality differ from individual to individual and each person interprets physical and social stimuli so that they are harmoniously accommodated within his overall world-view. This is accomplished by the individual reconstructing what he perceives so that it does not conflict with his basic attitudes, personality, motives or aspirations, or perhaps by modifying these slightly to allow the overall impression to be harmonious. An example of this process is provided by Allport and Postman.[4] When shown a drawing of a black man and a white man arguing on a crowded bus, and asked to describe it later, prejudiced people tended to recall that the black person was holding an open razor. In fact the picture depicts the white protagonist as having the weapon in his hand. The implication is that prejudiced subjects interpret the picture so that it is harmoniously accommodated within their existing perceptual field.

The Selective Nature of Perception and Attention

Each and every consumer in our economic system is daily bombarded with many hundreds of messages, each of which tries to inform him of something, persuade him of something, convince him, teach him or change him. Some of these messages come from sources the consumer trusts implicitly; some he rejects without further thought; but the majority of messages contain a mixture of obvious truth and doubtful claims that would require time, effort and possibly expense to prove or refute. Clearly no one has the time to evaluate every message that comes his way or even to give a portion of his attention to all that do so. One way of coping with the constant bombardment of information and persuasion with which the individual has to contend is through selection of what is perceived. As was apparent when we discussed the nature of interpreting stimuli in the process of perception, much of this selection is automatic as new perceptions are made to fit comfortably with existing cognitions.

A famous study of selective perception was reported by Hastorf and Cantril [5] who interviewed students from Princeton and Dartmouth colleges who had been shown a film of a controversial football match that had taken place between the two college teams. Newspaper reports of the game pointed out that there had been considerable amounts of rough play by both sides but that Dartmouth had contributed more to this than Princeton. Having watched the film of the game, the students were asked to say how many fouls each team had committed. On average, the Dartmouth students attributed about as many fouls to each team (4.3 to their own team and 4.4 to the other) while Princeton students, on average, attributed far more fouls to their opponents' team than to their own (9.8 compared with 4.2). Clearly perception depends on view point; selective perception means that, to some extent at least, people have the ability to see and hear what they choose to see and hear, to 'screen out' messages they do not wish to attend to or be influenced by or even consider.

The precise manner in which the person allows some messages to penetrate or 'get through' while rejecting others depends on his values, motives and attitudes as well as his social situation and current interests and preoccupations. As we have seen, messages which are in tune with what the individual already believes stand a much better chance of gaining his attention and being perceived than those which are at odds with his preoccupations or tangental to his interests and needs. The latter are likely to be condemned without a hearing.

Suggestions and expectations play a decisive part in determining whether an individual perceives a stimulus and the ways in which he interprets it if he does. Maier [6] shows that there is considerable variation in the perceptions of objects and figures depending on the suggestions which shape the observer's expectations. The following figure, for instance, can be seen as two X's, or as an upright V superimposed on an inverted V. If the suggestion is made that the figure is a W on top of an M, it may be seen as such. Maier also suggests that it can be perceived as a diamond with extended sides. The fact that the context within which perception takes place vitally affects the process of perception is of course of crucial importance to the consumer researcher and marketing executive. It means that the firm sells as many different products as it has potential buyers and it is the basis for some forms of market segmentation, though this possiblity contains within it the danger of product proliferation and 'false segmentation' if the segments are not sufficiently large to support profitable production which exploits economies of scale. [7] Selective perception also has implications for other areas of the marketing mix, notably advertising.

Perception and Consumer Decisions

Perception and Communication

It has been estimated that some ninety per cent of the stimuli individuals perceive come to them through the agency of sight; much of the rest comes via hearing. It is no surprise, then, to find that advertisements rely heavily on visual and auditory stimuli. But loud noises, bright colours and large advertisements do not, of themselves, guarantee that the consumer will give his attention to the message being broadcast by the advertiser. The use of haunting melodies, pastel shades, regional accents and careful adjustment of advertisement size in relation to total page or poster size all affect perception and, depending on the product being advertised, may do a better job than more aggressive or standardised methods.

Further, the selective nature of perception restricts the effects of any given advertisement no matter how prominently it is positioned or whatever sensory stimuli it incorporates. Someone who is currently about buying a house is likely to respond to all the advertisements placed by building firms in his local newspaper, giving them his undivided attention; if he does not plan to buy a new car for another year, he cannot be expected to give car advertisements the same consideration. Another reader, who is about to change his car but is momentarily uninterested in the housing market, may well show the reverse behaviour. Perhaps neither notices the advertisements for a new supermarket or those for shoes.

Because consumers' perceptions of advertisements are not necessarily identical with those of the advertiser, it is imperative that consumers' reactions to messages be monitored. The audience's response to a marketing message may be quite different from that which the marketing management of the firm which is advertising assumed and may render months or even years of marketing planning obsolete in the time required to show the advertisement. The phrase 'You're never alone with a *Strand* ' and the cigarette advertisements of which it was part have become a classic example of this but it must be borne in mind that all messages are to some extent distorted and misunderstood by some section of the market, simply as a result of consumers' filtering the messages they receive. As Drayton [8] puts it: 'The message broadcast by the marketer, if it penetrates the perceptual filter at all, will be modified by the forces of perceptual interpretation to conform to the individual's expectations.' Knowing how the consumer perceives his world and the place of advertising messages within it has become part of the marketing task.

All elements of the marketing mix communicate something about the firm to the consumer, of course, and it is not enough to get the advertisement 'right' while paying insufficient attention to the factors that complement or detract from it. Pack sizes, pack shapes and packaging materials may all affect sales through influencing the consumer's perception of the firm's overall market offering. Again there is scope for differences in perception between managers and consumers.[9]

Product and Brand Perception

Interesting studies have been made of the ways in which consumers perceive the products they buy and the brands they regularly choose. In particular, attention has been focused on the ways in which branding and brand perceptions affect the consumer's perceptions of product characteristics and attributes. Some of the tests which have been carried out throw considerable light on the process in which consumers perceive products. For example, Allison and Uhl [10] conducted an experiment to discover whether blindfolded beer drinkers were capable of distinguishing types and brands of beer. They also wished to determine the effect of brand identification on consumers' reactions to and evaluations of beers. They concluded that 'Participants in general did not appear to be able to discern the taste differences among the various brands, but apparently labels and their associations did influence their evaluations'.

These findings indicate that customers' perceptions of products derive from marketing effort such as brand images and brand differentiation in addition to the physical characteristics of the product alone; further, it can be concluded that in some cases those product attributes which are marketing-based may be the consumer's only guide to want satisfaction. [11] Thus all of the factors that impinge on the construction of a brand image must be examined in order to ascertain their effects on consumers' perception of the firm's marketing mix. In this respect, it has been established that consumers' brand preferences affect their perceptions relevant to housewives' perceptions of the freshness of bread. [12] It is necessary in this context to underline what has already been said about differences in product perception between consumers and sellers; even in packaging there can be considerable variations.[13]   A recent investigation of the reasons for product failure [14] shows that in most cases it is the product itself or its package which is at fault and misunderstandings regarding consumers' perceptions are undoubtedly responsible for many of these failures.

Price Perception

Perception has implications too for another element in the marketing mix, namely price. There is considerable evidence that for many products and services consumers judge product/service quality by price,[15] a practice which has implications not only for marketing management but for such aspects of economic and social policy as the distribution of income. [16]

Offered two similar versions of the same product, which differ only in price, many consumers choose the more expensive item. Such behaviour may be irrational in terms of basic economics but is easily explicable in the context of an affluent society in which discretionary income runs at high levels and social status is judged by levels of expenditure and conspicuous consumption. It is also explained in individual terms by the fact that most children are socialised into linking not only quantity, but also quality, with price. Naturally this phenomenon is not capable of being extended to all products and services; its very nature tends to make it exclusive to those items which confer status or which reinforce the individual's sense of ambition or achievement. Its domain can be established only through empirical testing and it remains an intriguing possibility for marketing differentiation.

A review of recent work on buyers' subjective perceptions of prices [17] leads to the conclusion that the price-quality relationship and the ways in which consumers conceive of it are by no means fully understood. It is clear, none the less, that the notion of demand being always inversely related to price has been dealt a severe blow. If price and demand are directly or positively related, the importance of pricing as a component of the marketing mix is greatly enhanced.

Another facet of consumers' perceptions of prices is the question of so-called 'psychological pricing'. In the United States, as many as four-fifths of food products may have prices ending in 9 or 5 and the use of prices which terminated in 9 pence or 99 pence in Britain is widespread.[18] The reasoning behind such pricing strategies is that consumers are likely to perceive a bargain if the price ends in an odd number; 'odd-pricing' is extensively used in cut price sales promotions to increase the feeling that a price has been drastically reduced. Despite the popularity of this method of fixing prices in some product areas (ladies' shoes, for instance), there is a lack of experimental evidence for its value in augmenting consumers' susceptibilities to buy. Especially where consumers attempt to compare prices and quantities from product to product or brand to brand, the practice of 'price psychology' may serve only to confuse the would-be buyer or its effect may be neutralised as consumers automatically 'round up' figures to facilitate comparisons.

A related area, though one which is not strictly a perceptual phenomenon, involves consumers' consciousness of prices. There is some evidence that price awareness is affected by socio-economic background. In studies of British housewives it has been found that middle class consumers were more ready to suggest prices for the products they had purchased than were their working class counterparts. The latter tended to be more accurate in their estimates of such prices, however, giving the impression that price consciousness is inversely related to social class. [19] It is interesting to note, however, that these results have not been confirmed in an American study which was replicatory. [20]

Store Perception

Various facets of a store or other business contribute to its image as projected by management and, more importantly perhaps, as perceived by its customers. Berry [21] suggests that there are five major components of store image, namely location, design, product assortment, services and personnel, each of which contributes to the consumer's overall perception of the place in which he or she buys. But the manner in which consumers perceive the totality of the business enterprise derives from far more than just the physical attributes of the organisation. Indeed, the entire range of intangible factors which are at work is so wide that it is unlikely that a customer's general image of a store can be traced back with any certainty to any specific factors. The precise influences of advertising, interpersonal communication, experience and so on that determine store perception are too complex and too closely interrelated to be accurately defined let alone measured with any great degree of exactness.

Customers' perceptions of stores are vitally affected by consumers' own self-perceptions and motives. In a well-known survey, Stone [22] isolated four types of store selection motive depending on whether buyers were primarily *economic* (that is, price-conscious and with limited spending power), *ethical* (shopping where they thought they ought to shop), *personalising* (selecting stores for the service and personal attention provided) or *apathetic* (choosing stores which were convenient but which had no other major characteristics which made them stand out). It is also clear from research that consumers' self-images — which will be further discussed in Chapter 4 — influence the places in which they shop. Thus, while wives of professional men usually buy in the same store as each other, few of them are likely to choose any stores in common with lower class women. [23]   Such results as these emphasise also the effects of peer groupings and social position on store selection and perception.

Geographers and planners have provided considerable data on the spatial aspects of consumers' store perceptions and a variety of models of consumer learning behaviour and attitudes has been put forward. [24] While none of these has proved capable of explaining more than a handful of the dimensions involved in this area of consumer behaviour, it has been clearly demonstrated that housewives are able to distinguish between stores that are friendly versus unfriendly, honest versus dishonest, modern versus old-fashioned, etc. [25] It has further been shown that store perceptions vary from class to class (higher status shoppers are more likely to rate supermarkets as lacking in friendliness) and that age impinges on housewives' images of greengrocers (younger women thought they were more dirty than did older consumers). [26] This whole field is showing signs of promise but is beset by methodological and conceptual problems; as such it suggests a fruitful area of study for an interdisciplinary team of researchers, behavioural scientists as well as geographers, since each discipline brings essential perspectives to the analysis of consumer behaviour which are likely to be neglected by others.

Gestalt Approaches to Perception

Gestalt psychology stresses the fact that perception of a stimulus takes place within a known context and that the individual's reaction is thus crucially affected by his general world-view. (The German word 'Gestalt' means 'whole' or 'entirety'.) No stimulus occurs in isolation from a host of others unless under experimental conditions when there is still scope for the individual's interpretation to be affected by previous experience and memories. In marketing this fact acts as a deterrent to the temptation to judge the consumer's whole image of product, brand or store, simply as the sum of its various components.

There are two important ways in which this approach to perception can be used to understand consumer behaviour. The first, 'closure', is by far the more vital. In closure the individual tends to complete

information (usually sentences or figures) which are presented to him
only partially. It is well demonstrated in the Schweppes advertisements
which included the phrase 'Schhhh....you know who' and has also been
used in colour supplement advertisements for men's clothes ('The
Powe Game'). As long as the example employed does not confuse the
consumer or contain ambiguous or esoteric knowledge, it probably
serves the purpose of making the potential buyer think rather longer
than usual about the product's brand name and thereby more easily able
to recall it. If, however, the type of closure employed is less obvious than
the above examples, the result may well be failure (Schweppes's
follow-up campaign based on the 'weppe' — an essential ingredient of the
company's drinks — had nowhere near the same appeal and seems not to
have been widely noticed).

The other application of Gestalt phenomena in marketing refers to
the tendency of people to perceive proximate objects or symbols as
definite patterns. Examples of proximity are:

and

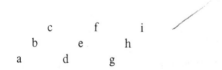

The first is seen as a series of diagonal lines rather than a pattern of
horizontal or vertical ones; the second is perceived as three three-letter
patterns but they are abc, def, ghi, rather than cfi, beh and adg. [27]
Recognition that symbols are perceived according to their position
within a larger pattern can have implications for store layout,
advertisement design and packaging. The principle of proximity, while
it is of analytical interest, demonstrates well the tendency of some
behavioural scientists to elaborate and add sophistication to marketing
phenomena which are adequate on a common-sense level for the needs
of practitioners.

Subliminal Advertising and Perceptual Defence

Perception that takes place below the threshold of sound, vision, and so on is known as subliminal perception. Attempts to use this in marketing have led to subliminal advertising, an attempt to influence consumers to purchase a particular product or brand without their being aware that any such appeal has been made to them. Its history begins with James Vicary, an American junior executive, who claimed in the late 1950s to have insinuated advertising messages into normal film performances and to have caused thereby a 57 per cent increase in sales of Coca Cola and an increase of 18 per cent in popcorn sales in the cinema foyer.

The public consternation that ensued is hardly surprising but the fact that subsequent replications of Vicary's experiments failed to produce comparable results is less widely known. It has even been suggested as an alternative explanation that the positioning of popcorn and Coke in the cinema foyer during the six-week period of the tests led to the increase in sales. [28]   While subliminal perception may be possible, it does not appear to operate in favour of those who would like to manipulate others. One psychologist [29] has written that the only people likely to be influenced to buy the product in question are those who would no doubt purchase it anyway and that the vast majority of people do not perceive subliminal messages at all. 'The whole idea of insinuating into the mind an idea which runs contrary to its basic trends is absurd', he writes. [30] The mechanism which protects the individual from mental overload and which results in selective perception also appears to operate here, and attempts to circumvent it through subliminal advertising appear to pose little threat to the independence of the consumer. In case there is room for doubt, the use of this technique is banned by the Advertising Authority's code of practice.

Use of subliminal advertising might well have quite deleterious consequences for the manager since consumers may misunderstand stimuli that are presented at levels below the normal thresholds of sensory experience. Barthol and Goldstein, [31] after a review of the topic, point out that the message 'Drink Coca Cola', subliminally projected, could be read as 'Drink Pepsi Cola' or 'Drink Cocoa' or even 'Drive Safely'. They conclude that consumers are safe, since 'we are staunchly protected by our insufficient nervous systems, our prejudices, our lack of attention, and the inalienable right to completely misunderstand, misinterpret and ignore what we don't see clearly.' [32]

Consumer Behaviour as Learning

Learning and Perception

Learning is closely associated with perception. Both involve the individual's responses to environmental and psycho-social stimuli; both can be explained theoretically in terms of either a stimulus-response or a Gestalt paradigm, both processes are intimately connected with and shaped by the individual's attitudes, personality and motives. Learning influences perception and, in turn, depends upon it.

What Learning Means

In behavioural science, learning refers to any change in behaviour which comes about as a result of experience. The concept rules out behavioural changes which occur as a result of normal growth, development or maturation, as well as physiological changes such as tiredness, thirst, or those which are drug-induced. Such a definition takes us beyond intellectual learning; the acquisition of information is but one aspect of learning in this context. Maier [33] adds the development of skills in leadership and problem solving, and the acquisition of constructive attitudes. A fourth type of learning which is highly relevant to consumer studies is the formation of associations.

Even the most basic elements of consumer behaviour are learned responses to the environment. Thus the housewife learns which supermarket gives her the best value and which food brands elicit congratulations on her cooking from her family and guests. The importance of this concept to consumer behaviour lies in the fact that all consumer preferences are learned rather than innate and that because of the nature of perception there is enormous scope for marketing managers to differentiate products and brands on the basis of attributes which the consumer learns about rather than knows instinctively. A great deal of present consumer behaviour depends on the learning that arises from past experience. Indeed, consumer action has been depicted as a probabilistic process which is influence by previous purchase experience and the time intervals between purchases. [34] Nevertheless, it is still far from clear how the various components of the marketing mix impinge on brand choice decision making and what behavioural factors mediate between the firm's marketing offerings and the learning process in the buyer. Definite empirical knowledge of this area is scant, despite the theoretical treatises of marketing writers, though the suggestion by Krugman [35] that television advertising may have little impact on the audience's learning processes as a result of consumers having a low level of involvement is worthy of consideration by marketing communicators and should be subjected to further empirical observation. Such low involvement in the content of many advertisements is a factor that commends the use of generic advertisements, those in which firms advertise not their particular products but show the general research they are undertaking and the benefits of their work on hospital treatments or agriculture (such advertising has been effectively used by firms like I.C.I. and Phillips to raise the general level of audience awareness in their products and to link their names with quality and usefulness.

The Rate of Learning and Reinforcement

Learning, whether it be of a manual skill in industry or of consumer choice patterns, does not take place at the same rate all the time. Periods of more or less rapid learning are usually interspersed with plateaux, times when little or no further learning occurs but during which there is assimilation and consolidation of whatever has previously been learned. Some advertising campaigns are thought to be more effective, therefore, if they are of limited duration (say two or three months for a television campaign) and separated by a few weeks or months from similar campaigns. There is some evidence that this applies particularly to new products and brands. [36]

Generally speaking, marketing managers seem to be concerned with attempts to increase the rate at which learning takes place and to reduce the rate at which consumers' memory decays. For example, several researchers have drawn on studies of the psychology of reinforcement. Reinforcement is closely allied to one of the oldest and simplest of laws that psychology has produced — the law of effect — which states that actions that are enjoyed or satisfying are repeated. Howard [37] defines reinforcement as 'any event that strengthens the tendency for a response to be repeated'. In everyday parlance, a reinforcement is a reward.

Now, it is obvious that a consumer who purchases a particular brand is likely to repeat this buying pattern only if he derives a certain minimum level of satisfaction from the purchased item. Consumers who are disappointed in their choices are likely to switch to alternative brands. For this reason, advertising and other promotional efforts must make claims which can be borne out by the consumer's post-purchase experience of the product. Otherwise repeat sales and brand loyalty will not result since the strength and amount of reinforcement are directly (though not simply) related to the number of behavioural repetitions the customer makes. Summarising other researchers' findings, Walters [38] states that there will be a higher rate of learning (1) with increased reinforcement, (2) when there are periods of rest between responses, (3) as the magnitude of the reward increases, (4) when rewards vary or are only sometimes given, and (5) when the reward quickly follows the response.

Consumers whose behaviour is followed by continued positive reinforcement form persisting associations or habits which may be difficult to break. A single disappointing reaction to a particular brand may not be enough to overcome all the reinforcement that has previously taken place, but it must be borne in mind that habits are not usually permanent characteristics of behaviour and that brand loyalty is a vulnerable facet of consumer buying. [39]

Summary

Perception, which refers to the reception and interpretation of external stimuli by an individual, begins with the process of sensation and is a selective operation. Without attention being given to a stimulus, perception will not take place and people give their attention largely to those things in which they have an interest, or which are novel, or from which they derive pleasure and satisfaction. Consumers react to advertisements, products, packages and so on according to their motives, attitudes and social situation and each individual's perception of these marketing mix elements is unique to him or her. Perceptions of store images, prices, brands and advertising messages may vary significantly from one part of a company's market to another. Subliminal and Gestalt models of perception were also discussed in this chapter and were found to have interesting but limited applications to marketing. [40]

Consumer behaviour is a process of learning; it is modified according to the customer's past experience and the objectives he or she has set. Learning is particularly associated with loyalty (to a brand or a store) and, in so far as this phenomenon exists, it can be understood in terms of the psychologist's learning theory. Marketing managers must take care to ensure that their customers receive positive reinforcement of their beliefs about a product when they come to use it, especially if these beliefs are based on advertising claims.

Notes and References

1. J.F. Engel *et al.*, *Consumer Behaviour*, Holt, 1968, p.79
2. C.G. Walters, *Consumer Behaviour: Theory and Practice*, Irwin, 1974, p. 138.
3. P.T. Young, *Motivation and Emotion*, Wiley, 1961.

4.   G.W. Allport and L. Postman, 'The basic psychology of rumour', in E. Macoby *et al.* (eds), *Readings in Social Psychology*, Holt, 1966.

5.   A.H. Hastorf and H.Cantril, 'They saw a game: a case study', *Journal of Abnormal and Social Psychology*, 49, 1954.

6.   N.R.F. Maier, *Psychology in Industry*, Harrap, 1965, p.23.

7.   W.H. Reynolds, 'More sense about segmentation', *Harvard Business Review*, 1965, pp. 107-14.

8.   J.L. Drayton, 'Consumer behaviour: the state of the art', *Proc. Marketing Education Group of the U.K. Annual Conference*, Strathclyde University, 1976, p.2.

9.   For an example involving differential marketer and consumer perceptions of domestic appliance attributes, see P.J. McClure and J.K. Ryan, 'Differences between retailers' and consumers' perceptions', *Journal of Marketing Research*, 4, 1968.

10.   R.I. Allison and K.P. Uhl, 'Influence of beer brand identification on taste perception', *Journal of Marketing Research*, 1, 1964, pp. 36-9.

11.   J.C. Makens, 'Effect of brand preference on consumers' perceived taste of turkey meat', *Journal of Applied Psychology*, August 1961.

12.   R.L. Brown, 'Wrapper influence on the perception of freshness in bread', *Journal of Applied Psychology*, August 1958.

13.   M. Blum and V. Appel, 'Consumer versus management reaction to new package development', *Journal of Applied Psychology*, August 1961.

14.   Nielsen Researcher, 1973.

15.   D.S. Tull *et al.*, 'The relationship of price and imputed quality', *Journal of Business*, 37, 1964.

16.   T. Scitovsky, 'Some consequences of the habit of judging quality by price', *Review of Economic Studies*, 12, 1944-5.

17.   K.B. Monroe, 'Buyers' subjective perceptions of price', *Journal of Marketing Research*, 10, 1973.

18.   L. Friedman, 'Psychological pricing in the food industry', in A. Phillips and O. Williamson, *Prices: Issues in Theory, Practice and Public Policy*, University of Pennsylvania, 1967.

19.   A. Gabor and C. Granger, 'On the price consciousness of consumers', *Applied Statistics*, 10, 1961.

20.   F.E. Brown, 'Price perceptions and store patronage', *Proc. American Marketing Association*, 1968.

21.   L.L. Berry, 'The components of department store image: a theoretical and empirical analysis', *Journal of Retailing*, 45, 1969.

22.   G.P. Stone, 'City shoppers and urban identification', *American Journal of Sociology*, 60, 1954.

23.   W.B. Weale, 'Measuring the consumer's image of a department store', *Journal of Retailing*, 37, 1961.

24.   For a survey of the important aspects of this field, see R.L. Davies, *Marketing Geography*, Retailing and Planning Associates, 1976, pp. 223-8.

25.   A.J. Bruce, 'Housewife attitudes towards shops and shopping', *Proc. Architectural Psychology Conf.*, Kingston Polytechnic, 1970.

26.   Ibid.

27.   B. Berelson and G.A. Steiner, *Human Behaviour*, Harcourt, Brace and World, 1967, p.151.

28.   J.G. Myers and W.H. Reynolds, *Consumer Behaviour and Marketing Management*, Houghton Mifflin, 1967.

29.   J.A.C. Brown, *Techniques of Persuasion*, Penguin, 1963, p.189.

30.   Ibid, p.190.

31.   R.P. Barthol and M.J. Goldstein, 'Psychology and the Invisible sell', *California Management Review*, 1, 2, 1959, p.34.

32. Ibid., p.35.

33. Maier, *Psychology in Industry*, pp. 17-18.

34. A.A. Kuehn, 'Consumer brand choice as a learning process', *Journal of Advertising Research*, 2, 1962.

35. H.E. Krugman, 'The impact of television advertising: learning without involvement', *Public Opinion Quarterly*, 29, 1965.

36. Myers and Reynolds, *Consumer Behaviour*.

37. J.A. Howard, *Marketing Theory*, Allyn and Bacon, 1965, Chapter 1.

38. Walters, *Consumer Behaviour: Theory and Practice*, p. 187.

39. G.R. Foxall, 'Marketing response to consumer loyalty', *Quarterly Review of Marketing*, Summer 1978.

40. M.B. Holbrook and J.H. Huber, 'Separating perceptual dimensions from affective overtones', *Journal of Consumer Research*, 5, 1979.

3 CONSUMER MOTIVATION

Perception of a brand, package or advertisement ensures that the
consumer is aware of the availability of a product. Awareness is clearly
a prerequisite of buying but naturally it cannot of itself guarantee sales.
Many people are well aware of the Guinness advertisements, for example,
and consume them avidly without ever thinking of drinking stout.
Consumer buying behaviour is motivated by something more than
awareness: it depends on the consumer's needs and drives, his tastes and
aspirations, plus his attitudes, personality and social environment. Thus
we cannot completely disentangle motives from other aspects of
consumer choice because the precise ways in which the individual reacts
to and satisfies his needs and drives reflect his predispositions, character
and experience. Some of the ideas psychologists have advanced as
theories of motivation are equally theories of personality, especially
those which are based on Freudian psychology.

Problems arise in the analysis of motivation because of the
interrelationships between so many conditioning variables. It is
extremely difficult to isolate the effects of any one factor. Motives are
usually inferred from past behaviour but the job of the applied
behavioural scientist calls for the prediction of future behaviour from a
current set of conditions. Since any single human action is capable of
stemming from many motives, it becomes necessary to decide which
factors have the most overall significance. Behaviour which seems in one
context to be motivated by pure altruism may, if all the facts are known,
be caused by avarice. Since the behavioural scientist is seldom aware of
'all the facts', perhaps because questionnaire respondents do not tell the
truth, perhaps because they do not know it to tell, accounts of
consumer motivation are almost certainly always incomplete. Sometimes
this difficulty is expressed in terms that suggest consumer behaviour is
only weakly motivated compared with other facets of human action. [1]
There is, however, no reason to believe that buying is in reality less
strongly motivated than any other behaviour – only that the means of
identifying motives are not yet as sophisticated as one would like.

What Is Motivation?

Motivated behaviour is activity that is directed towards the attainment
of a goal or objective. Two aspects of motivating situations are of
particular importance for consumer research. Firstly, there must be a

goal or objective which acts as an incentive and which is usually located outside the individual. Secondly, there is a state or condition within the motivated person which stimulates action, perhaps a social need (like popularity) or a physiological drive (such as thirst). A commonplace example which illustrates the connection between these two elements in motivation is the hungry man who experiences the hunger *drive* and whose behaviour is subsequently channelled towards attaining the goal or incentive of food (see Figure 3.1). It has been pointed out [2] that needs and motives are often treated in the marketing literature as interchangeable terms, whereas a person is motivated only when his behaviour is directed towards the satisfaction or elimination of his needs. [3]

Figure 3.1 : Elements in the Motivating Situation

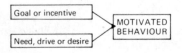

As we have indicated, not all motives derive from physical desires. Having satisfied their hunger and other physical needs, people may be found buying such items as fashionable clothes or sports cars. Evidently, the motives behind this behaviour originate quite separately from those which involve the satisfaction of hunger or thirst. A whole range of socio-psychological needs such as the desire to be appreciated or to have status stem from man's social environment.

Types of Motive

Maslow's Hierarchy of Needs

No psychologist has yet produced an account of human motivation designed specifically for marketing studies but a scheme that has been regularly cited in the literature is that put forward by Abraham Maslow [4] who presents the idea that there is a hierarchy of needs in man (Figure 3.2), which range from the physiological drives (thirst, etc.) through safety needs (e.g. shelter) and affective needs (for love) to the need for self-esteem.

The satisfaction of a lower-order need triggers the next level of needs into operation, demanding new patterns of behaviour on the part of the individual. Naturally the basic needs must be met first of all — to put it crudely, no one can be expected to be concerned about his esteem while

Figure 3.2 : Maslow's Hierarchy of Needs

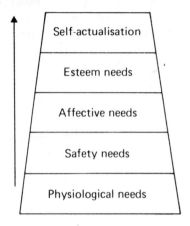

he is hungry. But once the bio-genic needs have been satisfied, the
individual turns his attention to the fulfilment of more advanced socio-
genic requirements. The final stage in the motivational hierarchy is the
need for what Maslow calls 'self actualization'. While he does not define
this term with any real degree of precision, [5] it appears to represent
the attainment of what other psychologists call *self-realisation*, the
process in which the individual has the opportunity to invest all his
talents and abilities in activities which he finds meaningful, activities
which help him develop his personality, e.g. through leisure activities and
creative pastimes.

There are many criticisms of Maslow's theory. At one level, critics
point to the behaviour of a hungry mother who deprives herself of food
in order to feed her needy children — effectively letting her affective
needs operate prior to the satisfaction of her own physiological needs.
More importantly for marketing, it is worth noting that while firms
provide the means of satisfying the bio-genic and esteem/affective needs,
the quest for self-actualisation, if it is a reality at all, would doubtless
take the individual into realism where the marketing system is not
necessarily able to assist. [6]

Nevertheless, Maslow's theory is useful in that it makes a distinction
between what may be termed physical/inherited needs and learned
needs. The latter are not innate but acquired by the individual through
social interaction. While marketing effort is highly relevant to the
distribution of products like food which satisfy basic needs, the
existence of social motives presents an additional dimension to the

marketing manager for all products and services. Firms may find it easier to attract consumers' discretionary income by making the most of non-functional product attributes if advertising and other promotional tools can be geared to the stimulation of socio-psychological wants as well as purely physiological needs. This is not new, of course — the contemporary pattern of marketing would not exist had this not been long understood. But if this classification of needs tells us little that is novel, it is a reminder of what the marketing manager must try to achieve and provides some confirmation of the basic tenets of modern marketing thought.

Freudian Approaches

It is more difficult to evaluate objectively the contribution of Sigmund Freud's theories and techniques to our understanding of consumer behaviour because of the bias shown by so many writers in this area. Some appear to have seen in it the key to all consumer behaviour.

It is certain that much of the sex symbolism employed in advertising is derived from Freud's emphasis on the human sex drive as a clue to understanding social and individual behaviour but no acceptable means of measuring the effects of such advertisements on *buying* has been published. It has been demonstrated, however, that when sex is not relevant to the product in question its use has no appreciable effect on sales. [7] Its use in advertisements for cigars (e.g. Manikin) appears to be related to the capturing of the (male) audience's attention; many more men enjoy Manikin advertisements than smoke cigars! So while there can be no doubt that sex is incorporated in marketing efforts, its value as other than a method of gaining the consumer's attention is highly questionable except where it is connected in some way with the product.

Another attempt at applying Freudian theories to the explanation of consumer behaviour involves his separation of the human psyche into three levels: the *id* (which contains our basic lusts and anti-social desires); the *ego* (the rational element which channels the urges of the id into socially acceptable behaviour); and the *superego* (a conscience of sorts which is, not surprisingly, in a constant state of conflict with the id). This is an intriguing account of the human personality from which some marketing writers have claimed it is possible to derive basic human motives which impinge on purchasing behaviour. [8]

Not all psychologists are enamoured of Freud; one [9] refers to this account of the human mind as the theory that 'man is essentially a battlefield; he is a dark cellar in which a maiden aunt and a sex-crazed monkey are locked in mortal combat, the affair being refereed by a rather nervous bank-clerk'! Certainly such an approach would have met little interest from marketing writers had it not been for Harold Lasswell's Theory of the Triple Appeal.[10] This states the idea that to be successful any piece of propaganda must appeal to all three elements of the mind; if it appeals to just the id, for instance, its effects will be immediately negated by the superego. This is advanced as a reason why advertising should not appeal only to pleasurable drives but also to behaviour that is socially acceptable. A Mars a day helps you work as well as rest and play.

Lasswell's theory has also been used to explain why advertisements which depict the romantic/sexual consequences of the use of products like shampoo or bath soap tend to end with the participants getting married.[11] This may well have appeared so in the 1950s but changing social mores have surely rendered this attempt to drag Freud's three elements of human personality into marketing at all costs obsolete. Recent advertising which invites one to 'Get into Bacardi shorts' or 'Join the Lamb's Navy' are little more than unveiled appeals to the id.

The major objection to Freudian psychology remains, however, the impossibility of designing an experimental framework which would satisfactorily allow the theory to be either confirmed or refuted. Clearly, not all that at first glance appears to shed light on consumer behaviour is of value to the marketing executive.

Social Context of Motivation

The specific factors that motivate an individual and the way he reacts to them depend in part on his social position. This suggests a means of investigating the relationship between individual and social structure through study of motivation in different social contexts. Surprisingly little has been published on this theme, a fact which may point to a general tendency in consumer research to draw rather bold conclusions from a single, almost classic case-study. The study in question was carried out by Pierre Martineau [12] who in the mid-1950s analysed Chicago *Tribune* consumer panel data and concluded that there were marked variations in motivation from one social class to another. (Middle class persons, for example, were more likely to be future-orientated, have urban identifications, extended horizons, a greater sense of decision making and a willingness to take risks. Lower class individuals were more likely to show reverse characteristics (see Chapter 8 for a further discussion of Martineau's findings).)

Although these findings may appear to have a near-universal relevance, they relate at best to consumers in one city in one nation at one period of time. If marketing strategies aimed at other groups of consumers are to be effective, they need to be based on more thorough analyses of the life-styles of consumers as predicted by both social and individual factors. Martineau's work provides a useful first step in the identification of such criteria, but contemporary marketing conditions indicate the need for in-depth investigations of the complex links between social class and motivation.

Cognitive Dissonance as Motivator

In 1957, Leon Festinger [13] put forward a theory of 'cognitive dissonance' which has had a considerable impact on marketing thought. Dissonance is a condition reflecting a tendency towards mental unease which occurs when an individual holds two attitudes, ideas, beliefs (or other cognitions) which are not in harmony with each other. In this situation, Festinger writes, the person tries to reduce dissonance — perhaps by dropping a cognition, perhaps by strengthening one. He summarises the theory by suggesting that 'if a person knows various things that are not psychologically consistent with one another, he will, in a variety of ways, try to make them more consistent'. [14]   Dissonance is therefore a factor in motivation because it leads the individual to change his opinion, attitudes or behaviour in order to reach a state of 'consonance' or harmony.

Although several interesting laboratory experiments have been conducted to demonstrate that cognitive dissonance can be engendered in individuals and to identify its effects on general behaviour, we are here concerned primarily with the applicability of Festinger's theory to consumer decision making. Perhaps the best-known example of a test of cognitive dissonance theory in the context of consumer behaviour concerns the post-decisional doubt expressed by purchasers of new cars. [15]

The existence of dissonance among such customers was deduced from their tendency to seek further information about the model just bought despite having previously considered several alternatives. Engel [16] has questioned some of the conclusions of others in this area; he suggests that dissonance may result only from price factors and explains enhanced readership after purchase in terms of the buyer's increased perception of the car's attributes once he has it at home in the garage or has driven it for a while.

Cognitive dissonance has also been evoked to explain consumer's reactions to the prices charged for new products when they are

introduced to the market. Doob *et al* [17] conducted experiments with
five products (mouthwash, toothpaste, aluminium foil, light bulbs and
biscuits) to test the notion that consumers who pay a high initial price
for an item are more likely to make repeat purchases than those who
pay a low introductory price. They explain their results, which generally
support this hypothesis, in terms of dissonance theory: 'the more
effort.........a person exerts to attain a goal, the more dissonance is
aroused if the goal is less valuable than expected'. Dissonance is reduced
as the individual increases his liking for a goal, and therefore it is thought
that the higher the price paid by the consumer, the greater is his
tendency to like the brand and become loyal to it. These authors
demonstrate that, in the long term, sales may be higher following a
relatively high introductory price. But, of course, there is always some
ceiling or threshold beyond which the price charged becomes
unreasonable and these results can also be explained in a way which
does not involve dissonance theory. Thus, a consumer who buys at a low
introductory cost and subsequently discovers that the price has been
substantially increased may show dissatisfaction as a result of confusion,
frustration or a feeling of being cheated.

No matter how the results of these investigations are explained in
behavioural science terms, they are important. Recent car buyers may
well need reassurance that their decisions were sound and this can be
achieved through advertising messages aimed specifically at them.
Indeed, without such follow-up they may select different brands in
future. Doob *et al.* use dissonance theory to cast some doubt on the
advisability of certain marketing promotions, but the fact that
alternative explanations are easily found means that cognitive dissonance
is far from being established as a marketing tool. Psychologists have not
universally accepted Festinger's theories as valid in their own discipline [18]
or have stressed that the notion of cognitive dissonance is very
complex. [19] Cognitive dissonance can, after all, be expected to arise
only when the individual's self-image is consistent with disharmony (a
deliberate liar feels no guilt and cannot be assumed to experience any
mental unease as he tells untruths). Intriguing as cognitive dissonance
phenomena are for the marketing man, therefore, we are far from
knowing the extent to which they operate in determining consumer
choices or how to exploit dissonance and self-image fully in the market-
place.

Motivation Research

It is apparent from the foregoing that the identification of consumers' motives is a complex business. The difficulties involved in discovering directly the precise motivating factors that shape buying behaviour led some marketing psychologists to devise oblique techniques for exposing hidden motives. These methods, known collectively as motivation research techniques, are concerned with a wide range of personality traits and attitudes as well as needs and drives. [20]

Motivation research may also be described as an attempt to uncover the consumer's suppressed and repressed motives (sometimes referred to as conscious and unconscious motives respectively). In suppression, the consumer remains aware of his motives but does not care to admit their existence to others for fear of ridicule, punishment or being ostracised. Information about the motivating factor remains in the conscious mind, however. Repression implies a more serious rejection of knowledge about a motive because the individual will not admit the motive's existence even to himself. [21]

The types of technique employed in isolating suppressed and repressed motives are well known and include depth-interviews, word association tests and projective techniques. It is not intended to describe these methods in any detail here as this is done in most textbooks of marketing research; however, several points are worthy of note. As long as depth-interviews do not degenerate into games of verbal wit between interviewer and subjects or into 'free association' sessions, they can yield useful information which the familiar questionnaire session is unlikely to uncover. Group depth-interviews all have the inherent problem of ensuring sample representativeness. Word association and sentence completion exercises can also provide usable, though obviously partial, and impressionistic data. Projective tests range from Rorschach ink-blot exercises to imaginary buying situations. They include picture story tests (thematic apperception) in which the subject is required to add a story to a series of pictures usually depicting a buying situation; and cartoon tests, in which a consumer is asked to suggest what cartoon characters are saying, or answer a question about the situation depicted, [22] may provide, for example, a picture of two women, one fat, the other thin; the respondent is asked to comment on their relative consumption of milk. Another form of projective test requires consumers to ascribe personalities to brands and to describe them as though they were living beings. (What is Mr *Daz* like? What does he wear? What sort of car does he own?)

The evaluation of motivation research is a difficult task. Early accounts tended to present it as a 'set of miracle tools available to plumb the depths of the consumers' psyche in some mysterious way'. [23]

A recent survey of the use of motivation research [24] reveals that it has now passed through its messianic phase to become 'absorbed into the repertoire of more mature research practice'. Marketing researchers and advertising men were partly responsible for the public consternation that greeted the claim that marketing had finally evolved tools and techniques to uncover the consumers' deepest motives and unconscious urges. [25] But the response of marketing writers to the critics who allege manipulation is indicative of the real usefulness of motivation research; for it has generally been pointed out that motivation research methods based vaguely on psychoanalytical theory and practice cannot achieve in a matter of minutes what trained psychiatrists often cannot do in years, that is determine the hidden factors that motivate an individual. [26]

Motivation research provides a valuable starting place for more traditional consumer research but it does not replace or make obsolete the majority of traditional techniques. Testing its validity (i.e. whether it in fact identifies the constructs such as repressed motives that it claims to) is a near-impossible task because of the inherent problems of experimental design and the use of control groups in research based (albeit loosely) on Freudian psychoanalytical theories.

Summary

The identification of factors which motivate consumers to buy is a difficult task because any given piece of human behaviour may derive from one of several influences. People may not be aware of their motives or may deliberately misrepresent them to interviewers. Thus, the nature of motivation is usually inferred from observations of the behaviour of others and this leaves much to be desired. Nevertheless, it is known that motivated behaviour occurs when an individual perceives a goal (incentive) external to himself and experiences internally a need or drive which stimulates him to reach that goal. Motives can be classed as bio-genic (physiological and safety needs) or socio-genic (affective, esteem and actualisation needs). Both of these types of motive are useful in marketing planning. Cognitive dissonance may also motivate. [27]

Maslow's theory of human needs is, despite criticisms, a useful starting point for the study of motivation because it involves the basic dichotomy of basic and learned (bio-genic and socio-genic) needs. Freudian psychology contains the interesting and potentially useful categories of suppressed and repressed motives. Lasswell's theory of the triple appeal is based on Freud's work but appears to have very limited application to the problems of persuading consumers through advertisements. Motivation research provides a useful starting point for consumer research but its varied techniques do not replace the more traditional methods of marketing research.

Notes

1.   C. Ramond, *The Art of Using Science in Marketing*, Harper and Row, 1974, p. 79.

2.   C.G. Walters, *Consumer Behaviour: Theory and Practice*, Irwin, 1974, p. 99.

3.   Walters states further (ibid., p. 119) that 'when a person *wants* to satisfy a need, we say that he is "motivated" '(emphasis added). Such a definition precludes unconscious needs which are, of course, of immense marketing significance.

4.   A.H. Maslow, 'A Theory of Human Motivation', *Psychological Review*, 50, 1943.

5.   Some of his critics have suggested that it means 'becoming more and more like Maslow'.

6.   The development of social marketing may be relevant here, however.

7.   M. Steadman, 'How sexy illustrations affect brand recall', *Journal of Advertising Research*, March 1969.

8.   J.H. Myers and W.H. Reynolds, *Consumer Behaviour and Marketing Management*, Houghton Mifflin, 1967.

9.   D. Bannister, 'A New Theory of Personality', in B.M. Foss (ed.), *New Horizons in Psychology*, Penguin, 1966, p. 363.

10.   H.D. Lasswell, *The Analysis of Political Behaviour*, Routledge and Kegan Paul, 1948.

11.   Myers and Reynolds, *Consumer Behaviour*.

12.   P. Martineau, 'Social class and spending behaviour', *Journal of Marketing*, 1958, pp. 121-30.

13.   L. Festinger, *A Theory of Cognitive Dissonance*, Stanford University Press, 1957.

14.   L. Festinger, 'Cognitive Dissonance', *Scientific American*, 107, 4, 1962.

15.   D. Ehrlich *et al.*, 'Post-decision exposure to relevant information', *Journal of Abnormal and Social Psychology*, 54, 1957.

16.   J.F. Engel, 'Are automobile purchasers dissonant consumers?' *Journal of Marketing*, 27, 2, 1963.

17.   A.N. Doob *et al.*, 'Effect of initial selling price on subsequent sales', *Journal of Personality and Social Psychology*, 11, 4, 1969.

18.   D.J. Bem, 'Self-perception: an alternative interpretation of cognitive dissonance phenomena', *Psychological Review*, 74, 1967.

19.   E. Aronson, 'The Process of Dissonancy', in L. Berkwitz (ed.), *Advances in Experimental Social Psychology*, Academic Press, 1968.

20.   Some authors have urged for a definition of motivational research in terms of any attempt at discovering why consumers act as they do. Motivation research would thus include direct as well as oblique methods, e.g. H.W. Boyd and R. Westfall, *Marketing Research, Text and Cases*, Irwin, 1972.

21.   Myers and Reynolds, *Consumer Behaviour*.

22.   H.K. Stecker, 'On the validity of projective questions', *Journal of Marketing Research*, August 1964.

23.   J.F. Engel *et al.*, *Consumer Behaviour*, Holt, 1968, p. 69.

24.   L. Collins and C. Montgomery, 'Whatever happened to motivation

research? End of the messianic hope', *Journal of the Market Research Society*, 12, 1, 1970, p. 11.

25.   G.R. Foxall, 'Advertising and the critics: who is misleading whom?' *Advertising Quarterly*, 48, 1976.

26.   See, for instance, J.G. Johnson, 'The consumer and Madison Avenue', *Current Economic Comment*, August 1960.

27.   W.H. Cummings and M. Venkatesan, 'Cognitive dissonance and consumer behaviour: a review of the evidence', *Journal of Marketing Research*, 13, 1976.

4 PERSONALITY AND CONSUMER CHOICE

The search for relationships between consumers' personality characteristics and aspects of their spending behaviour derives largely from the desire to segment markets psychographically. Segmentation policies derive from the possibility of dividing the consumers who compose the overall market into sections on the basis of some common characteristic such as social class, life-style or personality.[1] Other areas which have been associated with personality concepts are innovation and the selection of media. A quite considerable body of empirical knowledge has been accumulated which links personality traits and types with customers' product and brand preferences and to several other aspects of their behaviour.

Sufficient basic research has been conducted to allow several tentative conclusions to be drawn with respect to the usefulness of personality analysis to the marketing practitioner. This chapter is initially concerned with the meaning of personality as a variable in consumer choice behaviour. But since this book is intended as a practical guide to marketing management, it is also vitally concerned with the evaluation of this concept in a managerial context.

Definitions of Personality

The word personality is frequently used to refer to the capacity of a person for popularity, friendliness or charisma. In this sense personality is looked upon as a good thing to develop and many writers on popular psychology have emphasised that an 'attractive personality' is a necessary ingredient of success.

It is often considered an important element in management-training courses or public-speaking programmes. But whatever its merits in these contexts, this is not the sense in which the term is used by the majority of behavioural scientists.

Employing the term in a more strictly scientific sense, some psychologists have used it to refer to the essential differences between one individual and another. Personality, according to this interpretation, consists of the mannerisms, habits and actions that make a person an individual and thereby serve to make him distinct from everyone else. This provides a useful clue to the meaning of personality but it does not of itself add up to a complete definitional statement. This is provided by Eysenck et al.[2] who define personality as 'the relatively stable

57

organisation of a person's motivational dispositions arising from the interaction between biological drives and the social and physical environment'. Personality is thus a function of innate drives, learned motives and experience. The various themes in definitions of personality are brought together in Kempner [3] where the term is explained as 'that integrated organisation which determines each individual's pattern of behavioural responses to the environment', so that 'the study of personality is essentially the study of differences between people'.

Traits and Types

The meaning of personality in behavioural science becomes more clear when we consider the ways in which the concept has been operationalised in research. A dominant theme in the development of personality as an area of scientific study has been trait theory, traits being an individual's characteristic ways of responding to the social and physical environment. Examples are aggression, honesty, anxiety independence and sociability. Behavioural scientists do not consider any of these to be ethically better or worse than others; they are simply terms which describe a person's behaviour. By and large, traits are independent of each other and have to be measured separately.

Another approach to personality analysis involves the classification of various types of personality. The classification of people as introverts and extroverts is a well-known example which stems from Carl Jung's psychoanalytic theories. Another example is the model which emerged from the work of Karen Horney, [4] in which individuals are categorised as compliant, aggressive or detached. These type theories may be thought of as attempts to sum up a person's personality by referring to a dominant trait or series of traits. David Riesman [5] uses social character to sum up the individual's personality type. His sytem has three categories: tradition-direction, other-direction and inner-direction, each of which has implications for attitudes and behaviour.

Both traits and types have been explored as possible clues to the behaviour of consumers and any evaluation of personality's role in marketing depends on a critical appraisal of the empirical results which have been produced.

Personality Traits and Consumers

Two classic studies which attempt to link traits with product use concern the ownership of cars. Both were carried out in the United States and, among other things, involve car owners' preferences towards buying

either a Ford or a Chevrolet. Evans [6] cites as the stimulus for his
research the fact that, while mechanically and in design terms these
types of car were almost identical, advertisers had tried to create very
different brand images for them based on what they assumed to be
profiles of car buyers. Likely Ford owners were popularly portrayed as
independent, impulsive, masculine and self-confident, while probable
Chevrolet buyers were presented as conservative, thrifty, prestige-
conscious, less masculine and moderate. A standard personality test
(the Edwards Personal Preference Schedule) was used to measure these
personality traits and others which might be relevant. The test was
administered to owners of one or other make of car.

In a first trial based solely on the personality test scores of subjects,
Evans was able to predict successfully whether an individual owned a
Ford or Chevrolet in sixty-three per cent of cases, thirteen per cent
more than would have been the case in a purely chance situation. In a
second experiment, using only socio-economic measures of the
individual, they predicted correctly in seventy per cent of tries. In a third
experiment where a combination of both sets of consumer
characteristics were used, he failed to improve his accuracy beyond that
of his first try. Clearly, none of these results is sufficiently reliable to be
of much value to the car manufacturer who wants to segment his market
on the basis of psychographic criteria. A replication of part of this work
by Westfall [7] (which used the Thurstone Temperament Schedule in
place of the Edwards scale) also failed to distinguish satisfactorily
between Ford and Chevrolet owners by personality traits though it
succeeded in distinguishing convertible owners from non-convertible
owners; persons who scored low on measures of activity, vigour,
impulsiveness and sociability had a lower than average chance of owning
a convertible. Even this result is of limited managerial relevance however,
due to the decline in market demand for the convertible type of car.

Although cars have figured in a number of surveys, a wide range of
products and brands have now been covered by tests, as is shown in
the accompanying tables. Tables 4.1 and 4.2 also show that research has
involved a variety of traits. The results can be briefly summed up as
follows: there is a mass of evidence that personality traits are linked
with product and brand choice but the associations are, in the main,
very weak. Correlation coefficients of the order of 0.3 or below are very
common in these studies, showing that the proportion of variability in
consumer purchase patterns which can be explained in terms of
personality traits is quite small.

Table 4.1 : Personality Traits and Product Usage

Product/Behaviour	Associated trait(s)	Correlation Coefficient
Headache remedies	Ascendancy	− 0.46
	Emotional stability	− 0.32
Acceptance of new fashions	Ascendancy	0.33
	Sociability	0.56
Vitamins	Ascendancy	− 0.33
	Responsibility	− 0.30
	Emotional stability	− 0.09
	Sociability	− 0.27
Cigarettes	None of the four	
Mouthwash	Responsibility	− 0.22
Alcoholic drinks	Responsibility	− 0.36
Deodorant	None of the four	
Automobiles	Responsibility	0.28
Chewing gum	Responsibility	0.30
	Emotional stability	0.33

Source: Derived from W.T. Tucker and J.J. Painter, 'Personality and product use', *Journal of Applied Psychology*, 45, 1961.

It is true, of course, that no social scientist expects a single variable to be wholly determinative, i.e. to explain some aspect of behaviour without exception and without reference to other influences. As Kassarjian [8] states in a review of such research: 'To expect the influence of personality variables to account for a large proportion of the variance is most certainly asking too much.' (Original emphasis). This bears further consideration in view of the fact that the psychological tests which have been incorporated in studies of consumers were devised for use in clinical psychology rather than marketing research. Nevertheless, it is also true that personality trait variables tend to explain only five or ten per cent of the variance in consumer choice and consequently are of little interest to the would-be market segmenter. While it must be conceded that research in this area has employed research instruments such as the Edwards and Thurstone tests which lack validity in the marketing area, and that sometimes hypotheses have been hastily concocted, it is inescapable that trait theory is an increasingly discredited field of psychological enquiry. [9] Could the reason for the poor results in personality/consumer behaviour tests be that the construct itself is of little use? At any rate, the relationships which have so far been produced for both brand choice and innovation proneness [10]

Table 4.2 : Personality and Product Choice : Some Examples

	Product/Brand	Traits	Results
(a)	Fords/Chevrolets	Achievement, deference, exhibition, autonomy, affiliation, intraception, dominance, abasement, change, heterosexuality, aggression.	Allowed correct prediction of 13% more buyer's choices than chance alone would give.
(b)	Car Types	Activeness, vigour impulsiveness, dominance, stability, sociability reflectiveness.	'No personality differences between Ford and Chevrolet owners'. Low activity related to low convertible ownership.
(c)	Magazines	Sex, dominance, achievement, assistance.	Less than 13% of purchase behaviour variance explicable in terms of personality for magazines or cigarettes.
	Cigarettes	Dominance, aggression, change, autonomy.	
(d)	Toilet Tissue	Forty-five traits	Personality of no value in prediction of brand loyalty, number of units purchased or colour of tissue.
(e)	Private Brands	Enthusiasm, sensitivity, submissiveness.	Less than 5% of purchase variance explained by these 3 traits; other traits of no value.

Source: Derived from (a) F. Evans, 'Psychological and objective factors in the prediction of brand choice', *Journal of Business*, 39, 1959; (b) R. Westfall, 'Psychological factors in predicting brand choice', *Journal of Marketing*, 26, 1962; (c) A. Koponen, 'Personality characteristics of purchasers', *Journal of Advertising Research*, 1, 1960; (d) Advertising Research Foundation, *Are There Consumer Types?* A.R.F., 1964; (e) J.G. Myers, 'Determinants of private brand attitude', *Journal of Marketing Research*, 4, 1967.

indicate firmly that the successful implementation into marketing of a research framework, based on trait theory, is still at the stage of a promise rather than a reality.

Personality Types and the Consumer

The possibility that trait theorists have been looking in the wrong place for applicable information on the links between consumers' personalities and their consumption habits has led some researchers to substitute personality type variables in their marketing investigations. It is probably fair to say that while this has not of itself transformed personality research into an immediately usable management tool, the results have been more encouraging than those for trait research discussed above.

For instance, we might consider the work of Cohen.[11] He used the research paradigm advanced by Karen Horney (which has already been mentioned), classifying consumers into compliant, aggressive or detached types. Compliant individuals are anxious to be with others, to receive love, recognition, help and guidance. Such needs may make them over-generous and over-sensitive so that they shy away from criticism and allow others to dominate them. They are essentially conformists. Aggressive people tend to be achievement-orientated, desire status and see life as a competitive game. They seek the admiration of others through being outgoing in their behaviour and may exhibit what are often called 'leadership qualities'. Finally, detached individuals try to separate themselves from others both emotionally and behaviourally; they do not seek responsibility or obligations and do not try to impress other people. Each of these personality types contains sufficient unique traits to be conceptually distinct from the others, though in practice it is probable that many individuals possess elements of more than one.

In consumer tests, Cohen was able to match these personality types with product/brand preferences and usage rates. For instance, highly compliant people were more likely than less compliant types to use mouthwash, prefer 'Dial' soap, and drink wine at least several times monthly. Those respondents scoring high on aggression bought more men's deodorant than low-aggression types; they also chose 'Old Spice' while compliant and detached persons drank tea at least several times a week while the others drank it much less frequently.

Fruitful as these results appear to be, it is important to note that Cohen presents only selected data and that no statistically significant relationships were found for a wide range of products including cigarettes, dress-shirts, men's hair-dressing, toothpaste, beer, diet products and headache remedies. Nevertheless, this particular study tends to resurrect the concept of personality as a meaningful concept for consumer behaviour research. Preferences for media offerings were also discovered, taking the personality/consumer choice relationship beyond brand selection and usage rates. Aggressive individuals, for example, preferred exciting television programmes such as 'The Untouchables' and 'The Fugitive' and magazines like 'Playboy' and 'Field and Stream'. Compliant persons more readily chose programmes like 'Dr. Kildare' and 'Bonanza' and typically read 'Readers' Digest'. The detached subjects had more mixed and ambivalent preferences.

Social Character Research

A related approach to personality and consumer choice research derives from the behavioural categories put forward by Riesman in *The Lonely Crowd.* [12] This work classifies individuals as tradition-directed (those whose values and behaviour stem from the past), inner-directed (who have a strong personal sense of what sort of behaviour is correct) and other-directed (whose values, attitudes and behaviour are largely acquired from others).

Kassarjian [13] found that when presented with pairs of advertisements, one of which had a built-in inner-directed appeal, the other an other-directed appeal, respondents chose the advertisement which corresponded to their personality type as the one most likely to influence them. Both groups expressed the view that the majority of people were likely to be influenced more by other-directed appeals; but neither group showed greater or more significant media exposure or preferences. (As an example of the differences between pairs of advertisements, Kassarjian states: 'An inner-directed ad for a Book of the Month Club would contain pictures of book jackets about great people and adventures while an other-directed ad would contain pictures of books about everyday people, best sellers, and books on personality improvement.')

This experiment, conducted with American college students as subjects, ignored tradition-direction on the grounds of its alleged non-relevance to the American consumer. Tradition-orientation might, however, be of some importance to the understanding of European consumers' behaviour and even that of some Americans with respect to products of an antique or generally historical character.

Consumers' Self-images

Consumer researchers' interest in self-image psychology stems from the belief that consumers choose products that are consistent with their perceptions of themselves and reject those which are incongruous with them. Since purchased products also contribute to the development of the buyer's self-image, his selection of products and brands may, if this hypothesis is generally valid, be seen as an effort to maintain consonance and avoid or reduce dissonance. Two self-concepts have been employed extensively in consumer research: self-image (which refers to the entire way in which the individual sees himself, his evaluations and description of himself) and ideal self-image (which is the individual's perception of what he should aspire to become).

Several studies have demonstrated the general tendency of consumers to select brands which are broadly in accordance with their self-perceptions and with their subjective images of brands.[14]   In the case of cars (a product area to which researchers have paid particular attention), consumers have been classified as 'cautious conservatives' and 'confident explorers' on the basis of responses to self-image tests.[15] Each of these groups exhibited clear car preferences, the former for small cars which were perceived as convenient and inexpensive to run, the latter for larger cars which were seen as expressive of their buyers' outgoing, even dominant, personalities.

Owners of different cars also appear to have differing perception of car brands as well as selecting cars which are in line with their self-images.[16]   In addition, car owners also perceive themselves as being similar to other owners of the same brand of car.[17]   In another investigation, concerned this time with beer drinking, it has been demonstrated that beer drinkers had very different self-perceptions from those of non-drinkers (basically the former saw themselves as more confident, extrovert and sociable).[18]

These studies have several methodological limitations, however, often as a result of the use of Osgood's semantic differential technique (see Chapter 5). They have been criticised accordingly[19]   but their overall conclusions are of considerable marketing significance. A much more recent study[20]   which involved consumer preferences for a wide range of products (from beer to colour television, from art prints to snow skis) shows that consumer choices correlate highly with either self-image or ideal self. The evidence we have reviewed suggests firmly that self-image research promises to play an important part in future consumer research; of all the personality concepts which have been applied to marketing this one has probably provided the most consistent results and the greatest promise of application to the needs of business firms.[21]

Summary

Personality refers either to an extensive range of separate behavioural traits (honesty, perseverance and hostility, for instance) or to overall types of character and response (extrovert and introvert). In spite of some high hopes and *prima facie* evidence that aspects of consumers' purchase behaviour might be closely related to their personality traits, empirical verification of this association is still lacking. A large number of weak relationships have been discovered but it remains to be seen whether this approach will ever enable the majority of markets to be segmented psychographically. Type theories and the concepts of self-image and ideal self-image throw more light on the psychological dimension of consumers' choices but there is considerable need for further research before marketing practice benefits from these areas.

Notes

1. 'Market segmentation strategies attempt to take advantage of differential responses to a firm's actions by identifying groups of consumers with common response characteristics and designing advertising, products, etc. to take advantage of intergroup differences', D. Weinstein and J.U. Farley, 'Market segmentation and parameter inequalities in a buyer behaviour model', *Journal of Business*, 48, 4, 1974.

2. H.J. Eysenck *et al.*, *An Encyclopaedia of Psychology*, Fontana, 1975.

3. T. Kempner, *A Dictionary of Management*, Penguin, 1976.

4. K. Horney, *Neurosis and Human Growth*, Norton, 1958. See also Cohen, note 11.

5. D. Riesman *et al.*, *The Lonely Crowd*, Yale University, 1961.

6. F. Evans, 'Psychological and objective factors in the prediction of brand choice', *Journal of Business*, 39, 1959.

7. R. Westfall, 'Psychological factors in predicting brand choice', *Journal of Marketing*, 26, 1962.

8. H.H. Kassarjian, 'Personality and consumer behaviour: a review', *Journal of Marketing Research*, 8, 1971, p. 416.

9. N. Heather, *Radical Perspectives in Psychology*, Methuen, 1976.

10. A. Pizam, 'Psychological characteristics of innovators', *European Journal of Marketing*, 6, 3, 1972.

11. J.B. Cohen, 'The role of personality in consumer behaviour', in H.H. Kassarjian and T.S. Robertson, *Perspectives in Consumer Behaviour*, Scott Foresman, 1968.

12. Riesman, *The Lonely Crowd*.

13. H.H. Kassarjian, 'Social character and differential preference for mass communications', *Journal of Marketing Research*, 2, 1965.

14. I.J. Dolich, 'Congruence relationships between self images and product brands', *Journal of Marketing Research*, 6, 1969.

15. E. Jacobson and J. Kossoff, 'Self-percept and consumer attitudes toward small cars', *Journal of Applied Psychology*, August 1963.

16. A.E. Birdwell, 'A study of the influence of image congruence on consumer choice', *Journal of Business*, 41, 1968.

17. E.L. Grubb and G. Hupp, 'Perception of self, generalized stereotypes and brands selection', *Journal of Marketing Research*, 5, 1968.

18. E.L. Grubb, 'Consumer perception of self concept and its relationship to brand choice of selected product types', *Proc. American Marketing Association*, 1965.

19. E.L. Landon, 'Self concept, ideal self concept, and consumer purchase intentions', *Journal of Consumer Research*, 1, 2, 1974.

20. Ibid.; the full list of products investigated is: card table and chairs, country club membership, lawn mower, sun tan lotion, T.V. dinner, electric toothbrush, coffee, beer, wine, skis, adult games, dress-shirt, mouthwash, headache remedy, colour T.V., telephone, and art prints.

21. S.A. Ahmed and D.N. Jackson, 'Psychographics for social policy decisions', *Journal of Consumer Research*, 5, 1979.

5 ATTITUDES AND CONSUMER BEHAVIOUR

The concept of attitude occupies a central position in both social psychology and consumer behaviour studies. Applied researchers are usually not interested greatly in attitudes in their own right but as guides to behaviour. This is the position of the behavioural scientist in marketing. Unless attitude measurements help in the understanding and prediction of consumer behaviour, they are not normally of relevance to marketing research and management.

The Meaning of Attitude

An attitude is generally understood to refer to a predisposition to respond in a consistent manner to a stimulus, i.e. a tendency to act or behave in some predictable way. Attitudes are usually represented as being positive or negative, favourable or unfavourable to an object, idea, or other entity; indeed, Hughes [1] defines attitude as 'an individual's favourable or unfavourable inclination towards an attribute of an object'. Attitudes are learned or acquired rather than inborn in the individual; they are established as a result of the person's experiential and observational behaviour. [2]

The precise way in which the concept of attitude is used by behavioural scientists varies somewhat depending on their understanding of the components or elements of attitudes and on the work they intend to carry out. An attitude is often depicted as having three such elements: the cognitive element (which concerns knowing and believing), the affective element (denoting liking or disliking) and the conative (or behavioural) element which is the part corresponding most clearly to attitude as we have defined it (a predisposition to behave). Most behavioural scientists treat attitude as a multi-dimensional concept and this is certainly the way the construct has been used as a rule in marketing research. Despite the tendency of some psychologists to treat attitude unidimensionally (e.g. Fishbein and Coombes's use of the term to denote affective aspects only [3]) this chapter does not so restrict the term's usage. It is worth noting, however, that there are several difficulties that may arise in using the term in this way. The various dimensions of attitude may not always correlate with each other even in the same individual and since it is easier to measure the affective and cognitive elements there is a tendency to discover what the consumer thinks about a product while overlooking his overt behaviour in the market-place. It is therefore necessary to check whether attitude tests do in fact measure the conative or behavioural dimension of consumer behaviour; otherwise they are of very limited use as predictors of buying choice.

The functions of attitudes have been classified by several psychologists and sociologists. Newcomb *et al.* [4] point out that attitudes assist in the organisation of psychological and behavioural activities; Maier [5] states that attitudes determine meanings (by providing a context for the interpretation of new information), reconcile contradictions (by helping individuals to evaluate each other's opinions), organise facts (as in the process of selective perception) and select facts. Katz [6] attributes four functions to attitudes: the adjustment function, in which the individual assesses the utility of objects for the attainment of his goals; the ego-defensive function, in which the individual uses attitudes to protect his self-image by emphasising his place in his social world; the value-expressive function, by which the individual expresses his central values and self to others; and the knowledge function, by which the individual constructs the meaning of his world, or gives explanation to both physical and metaphysical phenomena.

Attitudes and Behaviour

Attitudes both affect and are affected by behaviour. In seeking ways in which behaviour can be predicted from attitudes, it is tempting to represent the relationship of attitudes and behaviour as a one-way association, thus

$$attitude \longrightarrow behaviour$$

but it is clear that, if attitudes are themselves influenced by past behaviour, the relationship must be more complicated; it is usually represented as a two-way process:

$$attitude \rightleftharpoons behaviour$$

Much of the work of social psychologists specialising in attitude studies has been based on trying to elucidate the relationships between attitudes and behaviour. Measures of attitudes often involve the sampling of opinions (verbalised evaluations of particular situations) and opinions are often only a rough guide to more general attitudes and a poor guide in the prediction of actions. A classic investigation of racial attitudes and opinions, carried out by LaPiere [7] in the 1930s, provides a graphic example of the inconsistency which may exist between attitudes and behaviour. LaPiere accompanied a Chinese couple when they visited hotels and restaurants across the U.S.A. In only one of some 250 establishments were they refused service and generally they found service to be above average. Subsequently, LaPiere sent a questionnaire to the management of each establishment visited asking whether they would be willing to receive Chinese guests. Ninety per cent of the 128 respondents stated that they would not; questionnaires sent to hotels and restaurants not visited also elicited a highly negative response.

Although there are many criticisms of LaPiere's study (he was a white Caucasian, for instance, and that might have affected reactions) it provides food for thought for researchers and executives whose work depends on the assumption of a high level of consistency between attitudes and behaviour. Fortunately, in many marketing situations it is sufficient to know that attitudes and behaviour vary together rather than to discover which affects the other; but it will be necessary to return to this question in the context of persuasion through attitude change.

Quantification of Attitudes

Testing or measuring attitudes provides the bulk of marketing research work as traditionally conceived. Despite recent advances into other areas, this task retains an important position in consumer studies. This section deals with several characteristic types of attitude measurement which are extensively incorporated in marketing and the related field of behavioural research. [8]

Likert: Summated Ratings

The method of attitude measurement put forward by Rensis Likert [9] consists basically of a series of statements about an object to which the respondent is asked to indicate his level of agreement on a scale of choices; thus he might rate each statement: strongly agree, agree, neutral, disagree or strongly disagree. For instance, the example in Table 5.1 is based on one provided by Newcomb *et al*.

Quantifying the scaling element in the Likert method is accomplished by attaching the figures 1 to 5 to the responses; an individual's attitude may thus be scored by summing his rating of each statement. This is a fairly crude attempt at measurement and it must be stressed that a score of $2x$ is not indicative of an attitude twice as strong as that represented by a score of x.

Table 5.1 : Example of Likert Scales

Encircle one of the symbols following each statement. A stands for 'Agree', SA for 'Strongly Agree', ? for 'Uncertain', D for 'Disagree' and SD for 'Strongly Disagree'.

If the same preparation is required, the Negro teacher should receive the same salary as the White	SA	A	?	D	SD
Negro homes should be segregated from those of White people	SA	A	?	D	SD

Indicate the extent to which you agree with each of the following statements by placing a tick under the appropriate number; 1 means 'Stronlgy Agree', 2 means 'Agree', 3 means 'Don't Know', 4 means 'Disagree' and 5 means 'Strongly Disagree'.

I think that butter is more nutritious than magarine	1	2	3	4	5
Frozen foods are more economical than fresh food					
It is cheaper to make cakes at home than to buy them					

Source: After T.M. Newcomb *et al.*, *Social Psychology*, Routledge and Kegan Paul, 1975, p. 497.

Thurstone: Equal-appearing Intervals

Thurstone's method of attitude testing requires rather elaborate preparation of a number of statements. A large number of statements which are favourable, unfavourable or neutral towards an object are sorted by judges into eleven piles, the judges having been previously instructed to place extremely favourable statements in pile 1, neutral ones in pile 6 and extremely unfavourable ones in pile 11. The intervals between the piles should be about equal. Ambiguous items, those the judges cannot agree on, are discarded but it is usual for the judges to agree on the positions of most statements within narrow limits and a scale value based on the median of the positions assigned by the judges is given each selected statement; the selection of statements is such that each scale point is adequately represented. The following examples are taken from Thurstone and Chave's scale for measuring religious attitudes: [10]

1.5   I believe church membership is almost essential to living life at its best.

2.3   I find the services of the church both restful and inspiring.

5.6   Sometimes I feel that the church and religion are necessary and sometimes I doubt it.

9.6   I believe the church is a hindrance to religion for it still depends on magic, superstition and myth.

The respondent indicates (by ticking) which statements he agrees with and the median scores of those ticked are averaged by dividing by the total number of ticked statements to give the overall score. The Thurstone method has been criticised on the grounds that the attitudes of the judges must affect their positioning of statements; while this cannot be entirely discounted, using a large number of judges (300 in the study of attitudes to the church) enables a greater degree of objectivity to be incorporated in the measure.

Osgood: The Semantic Differential

The method of attitude testing devised by Osgood, Suci and Tannenbaum,[11] known as the semantic differential, is designed to elicit subtle nuances of meaning which respondents attach to words or concepts and which are not normally identified by other methods. Pairs of antonyms are separated by seven spaces and the respondent is required to indicate by ticking in a space the extent to which he thinks the bipolar adjectives describe the object. An example is shown in Table 5.2.

Table 5.2 : Osgood's Semantic Differential

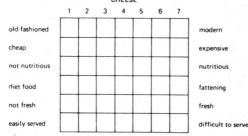

Use of semantic differential scales allows the marketing researcher to discover differences in attitude between different groups of consumers or of the same group about different products.

Wilson and Patterson: The Conservative Scale

Wilson and Patterson[12] have put forward a test of conservatism or authoritarianism which is basically designed to measure political attitudes. It is likely, however, that the dimension it measures is also of interest and significance to consumer research, especially in view of Graham's[13] identification of the importance of conservatism in studies of consumer innovation. Based on the assumptions that

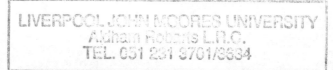

conservative people are (1) inclined to religious fundamentalism, (2) inclined to right-wing politics, (3) inclined to insist on rules and punishment, (4) intolerant of minorities, (5) conventional in art and clothing, (6) anti-hedonistic, and (7) anti-scientific, the test simply asks respondents to indicate which of a list of fifty items they favour or believe in. Table 5.3 lists the items;

Table 5.3 : The Conservatism Scale Items

1	Death penalty	26	Computer music
2	Evolution theory	27	Chastity
3	School uniforms	28	Fluoridation
4	Striptease shows	29	Royalty
5	Sabbath observance	30	Women judges
6	Beatniks	31	Conventional clothes
7	Patriotism	32	Teenage drivers
8	Modern art	33	Apartheid
9	Self-denial	34	Nudist camps
10	Working mothers	35	Church authority
11	Horoscopes	36	Disarmament
12	Birth control	37	Censorship
13	Military-drill	38	White lies
14	Co-education	39	Birching
15	Divine law	40	Mixed marriage
16	Socialism	41	Strict rules
17	White superiority	42	Jazz
18	Cousin marriage	43	Straitjackets
19	Moral training	44	Casual living
20	Suicide	45	Learning Latin
21	Chaperones	46	Divorce
22	Legalised abortion	47	Inborn conscience
23	Empire building	48	Coloured immigration
24	Student pranks	49	Bible truth
25	Licensing laws	50	Pyjama parties

Source: After G.D. Wilson and J.R. Patterson, 'A new measure of conservatism', *British Journal of Social and Clinical Psychology, 7, 1968.*

each subject is informed that he should give his first reaction rather than think about or discuss items; he records his reaction by circling one of: 'Yes', '?' and 'No' for each concept. Scoring is straghtforward: the answer 'Yes' to an odd-numbered item or 'No' to an even-numbered item scores 2; any response other than a simple 'Yes' or 'No' scores 1. The scale of scores ranges from 0 to 100.

This test is considered to be a highly reliable measure of attitudes but the types of words employed should be carefully selected and regularly updated as the meaning and relevance of items varies through time, e.g. item 6 Beatniks should nowadays probably read hippies or drop-outs. While the test is clearly useful for measuring conservatism in its present form, the methodology is so simple that it could be modified to deal with other dimensions of behaviour and attitude which are relevant to consumer choice behaviour.

Tests of Tests: Validity and Reliability

Users of psychological tests are naturally concerned that their test instruments actually identify and measure what they are intended to, rather than some other construct. No single test is useful for all purposes; no one test provides accurate results for all types of decision. Tests must be evaluated in the light of particular decisions that have to be made. Generally, a test is described as valid if it measures what it is supposed to measure. Cronbach [14] distinguishes four types of validity which need to be taken into consideration when tests are designed and applied. These are: (1) predictive validity, which refers to the extent to which test scores provide a useful basis for the prediction of behaviour or performance; (2) concurrent validity, which is concerned with the extent to which test results correlate with present performance; (3) content validity, which is a measure of how far a test item is representative of what the researcher is studying; and (4) construct validity, which refers to the degree to which test results can be explained in behavioural science terminology and conceptualisation.

Validity may be tested in a variety of ways, most of which involve little more than systematic common sense. Predictive validity, for instance, may be assessed by comparing test results with observations of respondents' subsequent behaviour, while concurrent validity is established through reference to existing evaluative data, e.g. scores on other tests which have previously been validated (there is a strong possibility here of circular reasoning to establish validity; validation confirms only that a new test measures the same thing as existing tests, not necessarily what the new test's originator desires to test). Content validity depends to a large extent on judgement and different research workers may disagree about what they think important and relevant. Finally, construct validity inevitably reflects the state of the discipline from which research problems are taken; really original research would require the modification of the discipline's paradigms and theories rather than the judgement of the test to be invalid.

Most of this need not worry the consumer researcher unduly since the majority of marketing research tests incorporate standard psychological procedures which have already been validated. It is nevertheless important that the researcher be satisfied that the test he uses is relevant to the research area he is concerned with.

Validity is usually expressed in terms of a correlation coefficient and it is comparatively rare for this to exceed 0.6. Evidently validity is a far from objective measurement but is at least superior to guesswork.

Another consideration to be borne in mind when a test is being selected for applied research usage is whether it produces consistent results over time. A test that does this is said to be reliable. Reliability coefficients may be established in two ways. The 'test retest' method involves the administration of two equivalent forms of a test to a group of subjects, after which the two sets of scores are correlated. Naturally, test subjects become more sophisticated at responding after the first attempt, and they may even memorise questions. One way of overcoming this difficulty is to allow some time to elapse between test sessions but if this is too long a period there is a tendency for the two sets of test conditions to vary considerably and this may reduce the effectiveness of the test for reliability.

The other means of testing for reliability, the 'split-half' method, also eliminates some of the problems of the 'test retest' method. It involves using one half of a test as a check on the reliability of the other half. Also called the 'odd even' test, it consists of a correlation of the scores to the odd-numbered questions with those of the even-numbered ones. Since the test is administered only once, there is no scope for using the method to establish predictive qualities the test may incorporate. As reliability depends on test length, scores have to be adjusted accordingly when the 'split-half' method is used. [15]   A reliability coefficient of 0.8 or above is normally considered very sound; using a split-half method, Wilson and Patterson derived a reliability score of 0.943 (on a sample of 244 subjects) for their test of conservative attitudes which was discussed above.

Changing Attitudes and Behaviour

A great deal of marketing effort is aimed at persuasion, which may be defined for our purposes as attempted attitude change and behaviour change. Social psychology has been helpful in this regard in that certain principles of attitude change have been presented in the literature of that discipline. Attitude change remains, none the less, an inexact science and provides an imperfect technology.

Attitudes are essentially stable structures and are not easily modified. Unlike motives, which arise from specific drive-states and are not usually long-term in their effects, attitudes are less specific, more persistent and resistant to change. Thus the first fact on which social psychologists and marketing managers agree firmly is that attitude change is a difficult and expensive enterprise. It is not an impossible one, however, but there is a strong necessity for marketing strategies which involve attitude modification to be firmly based on empirical evidence from the behavioural sciences. Since the literature of attitude change is so immense, the following discussion is selective and concentrates on those studies which have the greatest practical relevance to marketing management.

Credibility and Discrepancy

The magnitude and nature of the task confronting the marketer and the objects he is pursuing vitally affect the ways in which he may attempt to modify the attitudes of his existing and potential customers. Jones and Gerard [16] point out that most communicators have one or more of three objectives: (1) to create an attitude; (2) to change the sign of an existing attitude i.e. from negative to positive, or, rarely, from positive to negative); and (3) to increase the intensity of an existing positive or favourable attitude. The first goal is basically one which the manager is unlikely to have unless the product he is marketing or the need it fulfils is truly original; most are not. Thus the majority of marketing executives will be pursuing one or both of the other objectives.

Whatever goals he is ultimately interested in attaining, the marketing manager endeavours to produce the maximum of attitude change in his market given his budget and time constraints. The extent to which he succeeds in influencing attitudes depends on the credibility attributed to him as the source of marketing messages by the audience. Credibility includes both expertise and trustworthiness. [17] That there is a direct connection between the credibility of a message's source and the amount of attitude change the message produces may appear to be a common-sense proposition. Certainly behavioural scientists have had no problem in demonstrating the interrelatedness of these factors in experimental situations. Hovland and Weiss [18] showed, for example, that Americans were more likely to change their attitudes to believe in the possiblity of building atomic-powered submarines when a message arguing that this could be done was attributed to a highly credible source, namely J. Robert Oppenheimer, the famous physicist. Persons who were led to believe that the source of the message was the official Russian newspaper *Pravda* were very unlikely to believe that atomic submarines were a feasible proposition!

Advertisements which feature popular singers, actors, footballers and so on (for example, Henry Cooper's appearance in the Brut advertisement) are attempting to persuade members of the audience to ascribe the message they receive to a highly creditable source. If 'experts' endorse a product, their opinion appears more trustworthy and, especially in view of the fact that many consumers tend to discount much of what persuasive advertising claims, the use of a credible source may be crucial in gaining the audience's attention and in ensuring that selective perception does not cause the message to be screened before it is even considered. The exploitation of such methods of opinion change are limited, however. Hovland, Janis and Kelley [19] report that after a few weeks the positive influence of highly credible message sources and the negative effects of low-credibility sources is extinguished.

An associated consideration is the amount of discrepancy between the advertiser's claims for a product and the present attitudes held by consumers'. Some of the early empirical findings in this area appear to be contradictory. While some psychologists report that 'the greater the discrepancy, (between the communcation and recipient's initial position), the greater the attitude change, up to extremely discrepant points', [20] others claim that highly discrepant messages engender resistance on the part of the audience. [21] The apparent contradiction disappears, though, when source credibility is admitted as a variable in the opinion change process.

Aronson, Turner and Carlsmith [22] describe an experiment carried out among 112 female students which indicates that when an audience attributes a high degree of credibility to a message source, then, the greater the discrepancy, the bigger the subsequent modification of opinions. Conversely, a mildly credible communication leads to a smaller change in opinions when the discrepancy is great than when it is moderate (both levels of change are lower than in the case of a more credible message).

These authors also sought to reconcile their findings with those of previous researchers whose conclusions contradicted each other. They point out that psychologists whose work indicated a positive relationship between discrepancy and opinion change used highly credible message sources while the behavioural scientists whose work suggested that greater discrepancy led to resistance employed low-credibility sources.

Content and Organisation

The content and organisation of marketing communications also have implications for the modification of consumers' options. One of the recurrent themes in attitude research is the role that fear plays in persuading people to alter their opinions and behaviour. A considerable body of research findings relating fear to persuasion has been accumulated, as is shown by the recent review by Sternthal and Craig.[23] [23] Positive associations with fear have been found in the cases of dental hygiene, tuberculosis, smoking and car safety; while negative are apparent in the cases of fallout shelters, tetanus, roundworms and atomic bomb testing.

An early investigation of the fear-persuasion association by Janis and Feshbach [24] showed that, although a strong appeal to the motive of fear produced greater expressed intentions to act (in this case, the topic was dental health) than did moderate and weak appeals, persons receiving the less fearsome appeals were more likely to change their behaviour (e.g. by regularly brushing their teeth or visiting a dental surgeon). This seminal study has shaped the thinking of many researchers and writers but, as Sternthal and Craig have commented, [25] this conclusion flies in the face of the 'marginal statistical significance' of many studies purporting to confirm the negative relationship between fear and attitude or behaviour changes, and the fact that several studies have failed to discover any relationship at all. More recent research has generally led to the conclusion that the relationship is a positive one: fear persuades. However, there are qualifications to this generalisation.

First, persuasion through fear is closely related to the credibility of the message's source. The higher the credibility of the originator, the greater the amount of attitude (and, generally, behavioural) change that occurs directly as a result of the fear appeal. This seems to be the case because greater cognitive dissonance can be created when the audience believes that the message source is authoritative than when it is able to deprecate the fear appeal's origin, and cognitive dissonance is resolved through a change in attitude or behaviour or both. Where a low-credibility source is used, message recipients are likely to avoid the fear-inducing message by means of selective attention and perception.

Secondly, Sternthal and Craig show that characteristics of the message's audience may moderate fear appeals. Persons who are able to cope with tension do not appear to avoid fear appeals as do those whose coping ability is less developed; persons high in self-esteem are vulnerable to fear appeals as are those whose 'perceived vulnerability' is low – e.g. non-smokers or light smokers perceive themselves as having low vulnerability to lung cancer and are more easily persuaded by fear appeals related to cancer than are heavy smokers. Individuals who suffer chronic anxiety, however, do not appear to be more easily persuaded by fear than people who are not chronically anxious.

Thirdly, fear appeals are usually effective only when a means of escape from the threatened consequences is clearly depicted in the message. Failure to indicate how the message recipient can avoid the threatened effects of non-compliance with what the message advocates may simply result in the recipient's avoiding the message itself by means of perceptual defence mechanisms. This is important because it has been shown that threat of a social nature (giving offence to others or being ostracised) is more effective than threats of physical consequences. People appear to assume that horrifying things simply will not happen to them and are not easily persuaded say to give up smoking by being shown the physical consequences. It is probably easier in the case of threats of social disapproval to indicate to the audience how the more unpleasant consequences of their behaviour can be avoided. Despite the experimental and survey work which has been carried out on fear appeals, it is still difficult to recommend this approach unreservedly as the factors involved are obviously complex.

A consideration which also concerns the content and structuring of advertising messages is that of the one-sided/two-sided appeal. Should persuasive messages include elements which are unfavourable to the product or service which is being marketed? On the face of it there might appear to be no case for presenting potentially damaging information to any audience, no matter how sophisticated and educated it may be, for any amount of damage to the company's image or its brand images must surely result in lost sales and reduced profit. Despite such natural misgivings, there is fairly conclusive evidence that, within a specified context, two-sided appeals (those which incorporate arguments for and against the product or brand) may be more effective than one-sided appeals.[26]

The constraints on this technique are threefold: (i) the market or segment receiving the message must be currently unconvinced of the article's attractiveness (i.e. consumers who are at present not buying the brand and those whose current attitudes make them unlikely to do so in the near future are ideal targets for two-sided appeals); (ii) those most persuaded by the two-sided appeal tend to be highly educated (thus the academic practice of presenting both sides of an argument seems to appeal to those who have received large amounts of formal education); and (iii) the technique is advisable where there is a likelihood that the audience will find out about the less attractive (or even unattractive) side of the product anyway.

Much of the early work which supported the two-sided message thesis was carried out in the context of messages which, although they were persuasive, were of a non-commercial origin but there is now additional evidence that for a limited range of products (for example, kitchen ranges, cars and polishes) the two-sided appeal is superior to the one-sided message. [27]

A question which arises in the context of the two-sided appeal is: In what order should the messages be presented so that the positive one has the greatest impact? Even in the case of one-sided appeals it is natural to wonder whether the strongest arguments should be presented first or later, in order to have the maximum impact on an audience. There is no decisive answer to either question. The research findings to date are inconsistent, some resulting in the advocation of *primacy* (the first argument is the most effective), some in favour of *recency* (the latest or last message is most effective). Many pieces of research suggest, however, that order of presentation makes no difference to the overall message's impact. Engel *et al.* [28] point out that common-sense is also contradictory: if the strongest appeal comes first it may well arouse attention on a large scale but the weakness of succeeding messages may only detract from the general communication's effectiveness.

Some Other Factors in Attitude Change

The picture which is emerging leads to the conclusion that there are no general principles of attitude change which can be universally applied but that here and there behavioural research findings are available which have some impact on the search for persuasive methods which are suitable in marketing. Some other techniques and methods are in use and may be better known than those described above. This section deals with them and with the question of what theory has contributed to our understanding of attitude changes.

Repetition

The evidence in favour of repeating persuasive messages as a method of increasing consumer awareness and assisting, if not always producing, attitude change is impressive.

It is well known that the rate at which memory decays is very great and that an audience's retention of the information which is presented in a single advertisement cannot be taken for granted for long. Awareness of advertised brand names among an audience has also been shown to decay at a fast rate even after several repetitions of the message have been employed to establish it. There is considerable evidence for the assertion that persons who receive advertisements have higher levels of brand name recall than those who see no marketing messages and that awareness of brand names can be increased in an audience by several repetitions of the same message. [29] Even when a maximum level of awareness is achieved, some repetition is necessary to maintain this and if the advertising campaigns for some products are suspended and subsequently revived a disproportionate amount of advertising may be necessary before previous levels of awareness are obtained again. This does not mean that all campaigns must be continuous; it was stated in Chapter 2 that the rate at which consumers learn increases when there are carefully regulated period of rest from time to time in the receipt of messages.

In some cases, once a message has been regularly repeated often over a period of several months, retention remains at high levels for some months more but the effect seems to depend very much on the product involved. There is evidence that this works best when high-quality messages are used in carefully selected media and when repetitions of a single theme are incorporated into a series of advertisements which differ in specific content.

Nevertheless, there are difficulties involved in the measurement of retention. The only basic way of doing this is by asking direct questions about the advertisements, and brand names consumers have recently encountered, though there are several variations in practice in the way this can be done. When no cues are given to the respondent (a method known as the unaided recall technique) he is expected to describe all the advertisements he has seen within the last seven days and perhaps, depending on the interests of the researcher, to say where he saw them. This makes it difficult for the respondent to place his perception of advertisements in any frame of reference and the rate of recall is lowest using this method. In a different approach, subjects may be asked a more specific question such as to recall advertisements for a given product or product range (e.g. cigarettes) or they may be asked to remember TV advertisements rather than those appearing elsewhere (aided recall). In the third variant, recollection, the respondent is presented with a picture of an advertisement and asked whether he has seen it within the last seven days. This increases the chances of mis-recall since a familiar advertisement seen a fortnight ago may be recounted or the advertisement shown may be confused with a similar one. The errors involved in each technique may, of course, be minimised by using a combination of all three.

A great deal of learning and memory theory is useful in assessing the extent to which repetition contributes to attitude change. In most cases, repetition certainly appears to be positively related to consumers' expressed intentions to buy and these are often a good guide to purchase behaviour. There is always the possibility, however, that constant repetition may lead to boredom and psychological fatigue and that it may then reduce the consumer's intention to buy. The consumer's rate of learning (change in behaviour) is, as we have seen, related to the reinforcement through experience of the advertiser's claims and so it is likely that repetition to people who do not buy the product or who have had unfavourabie experiences with it may only serve to inculcate existing negative attitudes.

None of these provisos should be allowed to detract from the basic argument that repetition is positively associated with consumer awareness and that, at the very least, it facilitates attitude change. For many products, it is possible to work out an optimum level of advertising repetitions for the outlay involved and to ascertain the most effective rest periods between advertisements and, where appropriate, between campaigns. [30]

Role Playing

One method of modifying attitudes and behaviour which has been used with great success in some industrial situations is that of role playing. A typical example may involve managers, employees and union officials acting out a situation of conflict but taking each other's normal roles. A situation might be closely specified and even scripted to begin with or it may be described in general terms before the actors take up their new roles. This technique has been found to be effective as a means of developing attitudes which are consistent with harmony in industry: as Maier [31] says, 'in these instances real-life situations are simulated and trainees are placed in either superior or subordinate positions to give them the experience of approaching and viewing problems from different positions.'

The essential feature of role playing is that it encourages participants to take on roles which they otherwise might never assume and the success of the method stems from the changes it induces in subsequent attitudes and behaviour. We have already seen that the relationship between attitudes and behaviour is a two-way one and that attitudes can change if behaviour can be made to do so first.

The application of this to marketing lies in methods aimed at persuading consumers to try a product which they have not previously used, perhaps through giving free samples which the vast majority of people use readily or by means of any of the wide range of special offers, competitions and reductions which are used as inducements to buy. Changes in attitudes and intentions often result from such efforts where other promotional methods and advertising techniques are found to be ineffectual.

Theoretical Aspects of Attitude Change

The weight of empirical evidence discussed so far suggests that even the best-known methods of modifying attitudes are not infallible, although they offer considerable promise. Given this, it seems worth while to examine the theoretical aspects of the subject to discover whether more applicable techniques are likely to emerge in the near future. Day [32] describes four theoretical approaches to the study of attitude change which may be relevant to marketing; these are the information-processing theory, consistency theory, social judgement theory, and the functional approach, each of which will now be briefly discussed.

The information-processing approach posits the existence of a rational individual who processes the information he received in a logical, rational manner. Thus there is considerable emphasis in this approach on the way in which information is presented to an audience. That there is much to be gained by carefully structuring the presentation of arguments is apparent from the success of the two-sided message but we have seen that the order of arguments may contribute little to the success of a message. Day presents this theory in terms of a sequence of events each of which has a certain probability of occurring once its predecessor happens. The sequence is as follows: (i) the presentation of the message, (ii) the consumer gives attention to the message, (iii) he understands the arguments in the message and what he is being asked to do, (iv) he yields to this conclusion, (v) retains the belief and (vi) behaves in a manner consistent with the belief. The information-processing approach probably ascribes too much economic rationality to the consumer and does not explain the change acquisition of information to which the consumer has given little or no conscious attention or impulse buying.

Consistency theories assume that the individual wishes to maintain cognitive harmony and reduce dissonance. This has laready been encountered in the form of Festinger's theory of cognitive dissonance [33] as well as in the present chapter when it was stated that the use of a highly credible source may reduce the dissonance the consumer feels when presented with a highly discrepant message. The amount of dissonance increases in situations where the decision is important in economic, social or psychological terms, where several alternative outcomes, each of which is desirable, are available, where the alternatives are dissimilar and where there is no attempt at inducing the individual to make a particular choice. [34] The cognitive dissonance approach needs to be viewed as having certain qualifying constraints, especially the possibility that many situations of supposed dissonance can be explained in other terms (see Chapter 3).

The social judgement approach assumes that the consumer's attitude can best be represented by 'a range of acceptable positions [an acceptance region] rather than a single point'. Messages that fall within the acceptance or rejection regions of the individual's own attitudinal range are exaggerated in effect and marketing messages that are placed just within the region of acceptance are most likely to be optimally effective. Finally, there is the functional approach to attitudes put forward by Katz, which has already been described, and which stresses that different market segments may have the same attitude for different reasons (because the same attitude can satisfy several functional needs) and therefore different methods of changing attitudes may be required for each segment of the market that shares the basically similar opinion.

Some of the hypotheses generated by these theoretical perspectives have been extensively tested; Festinger's theory has produced literally hundreds of attempts at testing it in various contexts. Indeed, that theory is probably the most useful for marketing communicators though the cognitive consistency and social judgement approaches have also generated research which has been of some use in understanding aspects of consumer behaviour. Nevertheless, the problem with all of these theories is that while the issues they involve are directly concerned with many difficulties faced by managers they have not been well tested in the real world of marketing; so many of the research projects based on these theories have been conducted in artificial, laboratory circumstances and are thus of limited application to marketing management. While the theories are useful in the interpretation of some of the empirical results by placing them in analytical frameworks, they do not look like providing the breakthrough that attitude change requires if it is to be fully applicable to the day-to-day problems faced by marketing managers. Until progress is forthcoming in this regard, the empirical regularities discussed earlier will remain the decision maker's surer guide to action.

Alternatives to Attitude Change

Changing attitudes is an integral part of marketing despite its complexities and difficulties. Yet attitude change techniques may not be valid in all marketing situations. Less troublesome and less expensive methods of increasing sales might well be more appropriate than programmes aimed at altering attitudes which are central to the individuals who make up the market and which have been established and reinforced over a long period of time.

Marketers might, for example, consider changing the product or some aspect of the product to fit in better with known consumer attitudes and buying behaviour. After all, the marketing concept essentially involves matching the attributes of the firm's offerings to consumer wants which have been identified by way of marketing research. Therefore, to overestimate the possibilities of attitude change methods might be to become production-orientated and firms that rely solely on changing their potential buyers in some way before they can produce sales are undoubtedly not very consumer-orientated. Thus before becoming heavily involved in attempts at changing attitudes, marketing managers should ask whether they could not more easily attain their objectives by modifying the product or some other element of the marketing mix, other than the market.

A second alternative to changing attitudes is to reinforce those attitudes which already exist among consumers who are favourably disposed to the firm's product brand. There may be scope for increasing sales frequency or for developing new uses for the product. Associated with this is the creative use of word-of-mouth advertising which will be dealt with in the next chapter along with the whole subject of interpersonal communication. Denigration of the opposition has also been suggested as an alternative to attitude change but it should be noted that the only study of attitude immunisation which has been reported. i.e. reducing the positively held attitudes of consumers, suggests that such activity resulted in greater levels of beliefs on the part of the subjects. [35]

Even if attitude change is rejected as a marketing strategy, a firm must constantly monitor and measure its consumers' opinions and those of consumers who are loyal to other brands. Only by being aware of the current views of the market can businessmen decide whether action is necessary and, beyond that, what sort of action is appropriate.

Summary

Attitude is one of the most important behavioural science variables to have found a place in marketing thought and practice. Attitude refers to a predisposition to behave in a particular way when presented with a given stimulus, and attitudes towards people, places, products and things are classified as favourable (positive) or unfavourable (negative).

Attitudes are composed of three elements or dimensions: cognitive, conative and affective. Behaviour and attitudes are related and each may influence the other, but attitudes and behaviour are not always entirely consistent, and it has even been claimed that attitudes may stem from behaviour rather than vice versa. [36]   For marketing, it is usually only important that attitudes and behaviour vary together in some consistent way.

There are several ways of testing or measuring attitudes and some examples have been given. The instruments of measurement must themselves be tested for reliability and validity.

Attempts to change attitudes have included methods relating the credibility of message sources and the amount of discrepancy involved in the communication. Discrepancy may be greater when the source's credibility is high. Fear appeals also appear to work well when source credibility is high. Presenting both sides of an argument may induce more attitude change in an educated audience which is sceptical of the advertiser's claims, but the order of presentation of arguments does not seem to affect the response of an audience. Repetition and role playing also have implications for attitude change.

Several theories of attitude change have been shown to be relevant to marketing but there remains much testing to be done in real marketing situations. [37]   Finally, the possibility that alternative strategies to attitude change might be superior was discussed and while the modification of attitudes remains a crucial marketing objective it is not always the sole possibility or even the best. [38]

Notes

1.   G.D. Hughes, *Attitude Measurement for Marketing Strategies*, Scott Foresman, 1971, p. 9.

2.   See, for a discussion of this point, M. Sherif and C.W. Sherif, *Attitude, Ego-involvement and Change*, Wiley, 1967. For the view that there are innate aspects of attitudes, see W.J. McGuire, 'Innate and physiological aspects of attitude', in G. Lindzey and E. Aronson (eds), *Handbook of Social Psychology*, vol. 3, Addison-Wesley, 1969.

3.   M. Fishbein and F.S. Coombes, 'Basis for decision: an attitudinal analysis on voting behaviour', *Journal of Applied Social Psychology*, 4, 2, 1974.

4.   T.M. Newcomb, R.H. Turner and P.E. Converse, *Social Psychology*, Routledge and Kegan Paul, 1975, pp. 42-5.

5.   N.R.F. Maier, *Psychology in Industry*, Houghton Mifflin, 1965, pp. 55-9.

6.   D. Katz, 'The functional approach to the study of the attitudes', *Public Opinion Quarterly*, 24, 1960.

7.   R.T. LaPiere, 'Attitudes vs. actions', *Social Forces*, 13, 1934.

8.   For a more detailed guide see Newcomb *et al.*, *Social Psychology*, Appendix A: The measurement of attitudes; certain examples in this section are taken from this source.

9.   R. Likert, 'A technique for the measurement of attitudes', *Archives of Psychology*, 22, No. 140, 1932.

10.   L.L. Thurstone and E.H. Chave, *The Measurement of Attitudes*, University of Chicago, 1929.

11.   C.E. Osgood, G.J. Suci and P.H. Tannenbaum, *The Measurement of Meaning*, University of Illinois, 1957.

12.   G.D. Wilson and J.R. Patterson, 'A new measure of conservatism', *British Journal of Social and Clinical Psychology*, 7, 1968.

13.   S. Graham, 'Class Conservatism in the adoption of innovations', *Human Relations*, 9, 1956.

14.   L.J. Cronbach, *Essentials of Psychological Testing*, Harper and Row, 1960; see chapter 5.

15.   This is accomplished using the Spearman-Brown Prophecy Formula.

16.   E.E. Jones, and H.B. Gerard, *Foundations of Social Psychology*, Wiley, 1967, p. 435.

17.   P. Zimbardo and E.B. Ebbesen, *Influencing Attitudes and Changing Behaviour*, Addison-Wesley, 1970, p. 20.

18.   C. Hovland and W. Weiss, 'The influence of source credibility on communication effectiveness', *Public Opinion Quarterly*, 15, 1951.

19.   C.I. Hovland *et al.*, *Communication and Persuasion*, Princeton University, 1953.

20.   Zimbardo and Ebbesen, *Influencing Attitudes*, p. 21.

21.   For an account of these claims and counter-claims see E. Aronson *et al.*, 'Communicator credibility and communication discrepancy as determinants of opinion change', *Journal of Abnormal and Social Psychology*, 67, 1, 1963.

22.   Ibid.

23.   B. Sternthal and C.S. Craig, 'Fear appeals: revisited and revised', *Journal of Consumer Research*, 1, 3, 1974.

24.   I. Janis and S. Feshbach, 'Effects of fear-arousing communications', *Journal of Abnormal and Social Psychology*, 48, 1953.

25.   Sternthal and Craig, 'Fear appeals'.

26.   C.I. Hovland *et al.*, *Experiments on Mass Communication*, Princeton University Press, 1948.

27.   E.W. Faison, 'Effectiveness of one-sided and two-sided mass communications in advertising', *Public Opinion Quarterly*, 26, 1961.

28.   J.F. Engel *et al.*, *Consumer Behaviour*, Holt, Rinehart and Winston, 1973, pp. 337-8.

29.   Ibid., pp. 338-47.

30.   J.B. Stewart, *Repetitive Advertising in Newspapers: A Study of Two New Products*, Harvard University Business School, 1964.

31.   N.R.F. Maier, *Psychology in Industry*, Houghton Mifflin, 1965, p.74.

32.   G.S. Day, 'Attitudes and atttitude change', in H.H. Kassarjian and T.S. Robertson, *Perspectives in Consumer Behaviour*, Scott Foresman, 1973.

33.   See Chapter 3 above.

34.   Day, 'Attitudes and attitude change', p. 197.

35.   S.W. Bither, 'The application of attitude immunization techniques in marketing', *Journal of Marketing Research*, 8, 1971.

36.   M. Fishbein, 'The search for attitudinal-behaviour consistency', in Kassarjian and Robertson, op. cit.

37.   F.A. Johne, 'Positioning an industrial product using attitudinal data', *Quarterly Review of Marketing*, Winter 1977.

38.   B. Mostyn, *The Attitude Behaviour Relationship*, MCB Publications, 1978.

PART III : GROUP CONSUMER BEHAVIOUR

6 GROUP INFLUENCES AND INTERPERSONAL COMMUNICATION

The study of groups is a central theme of both social psychology and sociology and has included the analysis of human behaviour in both experimental groups and in 'real world' situations. Group phenomena are of particular interest to the consumer researcher because behaviour in groups is usually more easily predictable than individual actions. All of the individual characteristics discussed in earlier chapters — perception, motives, personality and attitudes — are modified by social influences and, especially, the social groups of which the individual actor is a member. A comprehensive interpretation of consumer behaviour would therefore be incomplete without consideration of the social context within which consumer behaviour takes place. This chapter is concerned with the informal groups to which consumers belong and with the patterns of interpersonal communication which occur in such groups. Later chapters will deal with the family, which is a very influential group as far as consumer choice is concerned, and with aggregate group behaviour such as that which is influenced by social class.

The Meaning of Groups

Although the concept of the group has a crucial place in consumer research, there remains considerable confusion about the meaning of the terms which denote group phenomena in the marketing literature. This seems an appropriate area in which to return to the basic disciplines of psychology and sociology to obtain more exact definitions and descriptions of the terms involved.

In everyday conversation the word 'group' is capable of denoting any collection of human beings, from one the size of a football team to one as large as a football crowd or even a nation. It should come as no surprise to find that behavioural scientists insist on a more precise definition of the term 'group' and that, used in the context of behavioural science, the concept has a rather specific connotation. Sprott [1] writes that a group is 'a plurality of persons who interact with one another in a given context more than they interact with anyone else. The basic notion is relatively exclusive interaction in a certain context'. In essence, a human group involves several persons who share common goals or purposes and who interact in pursuance of these objectives; each member of the group is perceived by others as a group member and all members are bound together by patterns and networks of interaction over time. The interdependence of group members is made enduring by the evolution of a group ideology which cements the beliefs, values, and attributes and norms of the group. [2]

Behavioural scientists also refer to *primary* groups and *secondary* groups. Primary groups are characterised by their size and by the close relationships that take place within them. As Homans [3] says,

> We mean by a group a number of persons who communicate with one another often over a span of time, and who are few enough so that each person is able to communicate with all the others, not at second-hand, through other people, but face-to-face. Sociologists call this the primary group. A chance meeting of casual acquaintances does not count.......

Examples of primary groups are the family, a neighbourhood bridge club and a work group within industry.

Secondary groups are made up of more than one primary group and examples are trade unions, a students' union, the social system of a factory and a school. Our emphasis in this chapter is on primary groups but it is worth noting that all primary groups are formed within the context of a wider social environment and interact with that environment. Further, primary groups may contribute to the achievement of the goals of the secondary group of which they are a part or may be organised so as to cause confusion and to obstruct the work of the secondary grouping. Consumer research is normally concerned with *informal* groups which occur 'spontaneously' on the basis of common interests and the geographical closeness of members rather than with *formal* groups which are usually officially organised groups with a more rigid structure. Informal organisation occurs, however, within formal organisations and is inevitably influenced by the 'official' structure of its environment.

Reference Groups

A construct which has been employed to explain a wide range of human behaviour and which emerges as the most important group notion in marketing is that of the *reference* group. Again, however, there is confusion in the marketing literature over how the term should be employed. [4]   General usage confines the term to any groups of people whom the individual uses as a source of attitudes, beliefs, values or behaviour (a single person who carries out this function is also known as a reference *group*). Three distinct uses of the term reference group can be traced in the sociological literature and all of them are useful in marketing research. They are:

1. groups with those members the individual compares himself, his attitudes, his behaviour, his performance;
2. groups to which the individual aspires to belong; and
3. groups whose social perspectives are assumed by the individual as a framework of reference for his own actions.[5]

The implications of reference group behaviour for buying are very considerable and we shall return to this concept later to assess the empirical evidence for its validity as a marketing construct. In addition, we shall consider some of the recent extensions of the basic concept which include negative reference groups and distant groups which act as reference points.

Group Effects and Group Dynamics

It is commonplace to remark that group membership involves the individual in the acceptance of a degree of conformity and that the group itself evolves norms of behaviour which specify the ideal actions to which members should conform. Social groups also tend to have a system of rewards and sanctions through which adherence to group norms is reinforced positively and thereby encouraged and deviance is punished and thus discouraged. Utlimately groups may exclude members who flaunt the norms which other group members accept and to which they conform.

Several interesting experiments have shown that, under laboratory conditions at least, individuals tend to shape their judgements so that they fit in with the opinions and behaviour of others. Asch [6] reports a series of tests which relate expressed opinions to social pressure and which confirm that there is a strong desire in most people to conform to group judgements. Groups of about eight people were asked to match a single line on one white card with a line of similar length on another card which contained several lines. Each member of the group selected the corresponding line individually in a prearranged order. All of the group members except the last to report his answer were working for the experimenter, however, and gave patently false answers. The point of the experiments was to ascertain the reaction of the final group member to report — he alone was the subject of the tests. He could either trust his senses and refuse to conform with the majority or he could go along with the rest of the group despite the evidence of his visual sense.

In almost thirty-seven per cent of cases, subjects chose to conform to group pressures and answer that a line which in fact was clearly unequal to the reference line was the right one. This occurred despite the fact that in control tests where no groups contained stooges and where no one was under any pressure to do anything other than what his senses suggested, less than one per cent of cases resulted in mistakes being made.

Individual subjects varied considerably; some were willing to conform all the time to group pressures while others consistently refused to do so, and few subjects changed their minds after showing initial conformity or independence. Further trials were conducted to find out whether the size of the majority was more important than its unanimity. Groups ranging from two persons to fifteen were used in these tests but beyond a group size of three increases in size had little further effect on conformity. Whatever the group's size though, the presence of a disturbing element — another person in league with the experimenter who chose to disagree with the majority, sometimes agreeing with the subject, sometimes not — reduced the majority of a great deal of its power and made it easier for the subject to disagree with the group.

A more dramatic demonstration of the fact that people will conform to the pattern of behaviour demanded by their role derives from the work of Milgram [7] who showed that subjects were willing to inflict electric shocks of up to 450 volts on other (supposed) subjects. In what was ostensibly a study of learning and memory, subjects took the role of 'teacher' and demanded answers to verbal test questions from 'students' who were wired up to a machine said by the experimenter to be capable of producing electric shocks. Despite the initial protests of the student (each of whom was a stooge working for the experimenter) about his having heart trouble, the majority of subjects playing the 'teacher' role proved willing to administer shocks for wrong answers. In sixty-five per cent of cases, the 'teachers' were prepared to give shocks of 450 volts (twenty-six out of forty subjects went to this level). Variations of the experimental procedure produced these results:

1. Basic test, subject
    unable to see student   —   65 per cent continued to 450 volt
                                    level

2. Basic test + student
    cries out   —   62.5 per cent continued to 450
                                    volt level

3. Basic test + sight
    of student   —   40 per cent continued to 450
              volt level

4. Basic test but
    experimenter holds
    down hand of
    subject forcing him
    to give shock   —   33 per cent continued to 450 volt
              level

Surprising as these results may be, they relate only to behaviour under closely specified laboratory conditions and it is not valid to draw too extreme a conclusion from them about human nature. Other experiments have confirmed these results, however, and there is no doubt that the tendency to conform exists outside the laboratory as well as inside it. But alternative patterns of behaviour are easier to find in most 'real world' situations and the possibility of an individual's being intimidated by the authority figure of the experimenter does not apply. Thus, while expecting group members to show fairly high degrees of conformity in the real world, we should not expect absolute adherence to group norms.

Sociometry

Conformity is not the only dimension of group dynamics that has interested social researchers. Group cohesiveness has also attracted attention. Cohesiveness has been described as 'the overall level of attraction towards the group' which 'can be equated with "loyalty" '. [8] It is this factor of cohesiveness which makes a group something more than a mere collection of individuals; it involves feelings of belongingness and integrity, and develops as the group fulfils the interpersonal needs of its members. Cohesiveness is also closely connected with the affective nature of the group and this suggests a method of measuring cohesiveness in terms of the likings and dislikings of one member for the rest of the group. Moreno [9] introduced the method of *sociometry* to measure cohesiveness in groups; this method essentially involves asking group members which other person(s) he or she would prefer to share some activity with or to select those who would surely be unsuitable for that activity.

Specific rules, laid down by Moreno, guide the process of obtaining this information; they include: (1) the choice must be made from a limited group of persons; (2) an unlimited number of choices should be given to each subject; (3) choices refer to definite activities; and (4) choices are private. [10] From the responses it is possible to construct a *sociogram*. The sociogram in Figure 6.1 indicates at (3) a 'star', a popular individual with whom everyone wishes to interact, and an 'isolate' at (4),   an individual with whom no one wishes to interact in the context specified. The triangle formed by (1), (2) and (3) represents a clique.

Figure 6.1 : A Sociogram

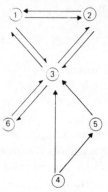

Source: M. Argyle, *Social
Interaction*, Methuen, 1969, p. 237.

The idea of group cohesiveness has not been extensively used in consumer research but, as the next section on Groups of Consumers will show, it has been demonstrated to be a valid concept for the prediction of consumer choices.

Leadership

The third and final facet of group dynamics which is useful for marketing research is the evolution of positions of leadership within groups and the formation of hierarchies. Leaders are usually defined as those who most frequently initiate action within the group, though this activity must, of course, be clearly relevant to the goals of the group whether formal or informal. Argyle [11]   comments that the emergence of hierarchies in groups is a universal human phenomenon and that whatever the size of the group some people communicate more than others. Other group members, perhaps less sure of their opinions, tend to look to the leader for ideas and inspiration. The person with most ideas, and who puts them forward persuasively, inevitably assumes a position in the hierarchy which reflects this while others delegate the propagation of ideas to him or her. Leadership may also be based on popularity and there is a tendency for the 'best-liked group member' to have some degree of leadership. In this case, he or she is then instrumental in releasing tensions, and questioning the role of the group and its members.

Groups of Consumers

Groups have been shown to exert a strong influence on patterns of
buyer behaviour and, in particular, to affect brand preferences.
Conformity to group norms or to the pattern of behaviour manifested
by the group's leader seem to be integral aspects of consumer groups.
The studies which are described below confirm the importance of
conformity, cohesiveness and leadership as elements of group
dynamics which are relevant in consumer research.

Cohesiveness and Leadership

In the mid-1960s, Stafford [12] carried out an experiment involving ten
readily existing groups of housewives each with approximately four
members. The groups were ranked on the basis of cohesiveness tests
from one to ten, the first group being the most cohesive, the tenth, the
least. The housewives were asked to select one of four brands of bread
over a period of time and to obtain all of their bread from the source
indicated by the experimenter. The four 'brands' of bread were, in
reality, identical save that their wrappers were identified by a single
letter of the alphabet: H, L, M or P. Analysis of the housewives' choices
at the end of the experimental period indicated that the group's
favourite brand was identical with the leader's best-liked brand for the
five most cohesive groups. After that, the relationship broke down but
the study demonstrates the influence of the group and its leader and
suggests that this is strongest where loyalty and belongingness are
highest. Although this was an experimental test, the housewives were
unaware of the nature of the test, and the conclusion that primary
groups affect brand choice appears to be a valid one.

Conformity and Independence

While conformity is an inevitable feature of social groups, absolute
compliance is never found. Independence is also a valued trait for many
people. Even in buying situations where people choose the same brands
of a product as their friends, they often select an alternative colour or
display their independence in some other way. The motive which is
responsible for this desire to maintain freedom has been called
'reactance' and there is experimental evidence to suggest that, where
compliance is forced, individuals will do their best to achieve some
degree of autonomy and independence. [13]

Venkatesan [14] conducted an experimental study of consumer
behaviour which was intended to throw light on the questions of
conformity to social pressure and the possibilities of reactance occurring

in consumer decision making situations. One hundred and forty-four college students were asked to select and evaluate one of three men's suits which were identical in style, colour and size and which were denoted simply by letters of the alphabet: A, B and C. Information provided for the subjects included the suggestions that the suits were from different manufacturers, that there were differentials in quality from one suit to another, that previous studies carried out at a prestigious research centre had established that the best suit could be identified by experts, and that the study in which the subjects were taking part was to determine whether buyers were capable of selecting the best suit.

For purposes of comparison, three experimental conditions were created:

Condition I
involved a control group in which subjects evaluated the suits independently, reported separately on them, and received no group pressures to conform or comply.

Condition II
involved groups of four subjects three of whom were in league with the experimenter. The seating arrangements were manipulated so that the confederates reported first, orally, that the best suit was B, thus establishing a group norm for the naive subject to conform to or reject.

Condition III
was similar to Condition II but there was an attempt by the experimenter at engineering reactance and the responses of the three confederates in each group were accordingly specified thus:

> 'Confederate 1: I am not sure if there is a difference — it is not great; but if I have to choose, then B is the *best* suit.
> Confederate 2: (Looking at Confederate 1) You say B.... Well, I cannot see any difference either — I will 'go along with you' — B is the *best* suit for me.
> Confederate 3: Well, you guys chose B. Although I am not sure, I am *just going along* to be a good guy. I choose B too.'

When it came to the real subject's turn, the situation had already been structured to as to reduce his choice.

The results, which are displayed in Figure 6.2, are consistent with the hypothesis that consumers generally conform to group norms when making brand choices but reject attempts at inducing them to make particular brand decisions.

Figure 6.2 : Conformity and Independence in Consumer Choice

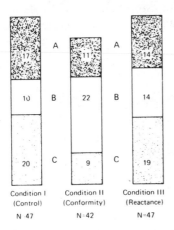

In Condition I, where no social influence attempt was made, the distribution of responses did not differ from what change would have predicted by a significant amount. In Condition II, where conformity was promoted, the proportion of choices cast in favour of suit B was greater by a significant amount than chance would suggest (i.e. than one third) which indicates that conformity to a group norm is to be expected. However, in Condition III, where compliance was induced, the proportion of choices of suit B was not significantly different from one third, indicating that consumers who realise they are being forced to conform to the group's standards may react by deliberately asserting their independence.

Reference Groups and Consumer Behaviour

Both of the studies discussed so far have involved reference group phenomena but in each case the reference group in question was also a membership group for the subjects. An analysis of reference group behaviour and consumption which provides a framework suitable for studying the reference point effects of non-membership groups has been put forward by Bourne. [15]   He and his colleagues at the Foundation for Research on Human Behaviour identified conspicuousness as the most pervasive product attribute involved in reference group influence. Conspicuousness, however, can mean two things: not only must the product be capable of being seen and perceived by others; it must also stand out and command attention.

Bourne recognised that the influence of reference groups varies from product to product and set out to isolate those product areas where reference group influence was particularly strong. He claimed that the strongest influence occurred in relation to those products and brands about which people had evolved strong norms specifying ideal behaviour on usage patterns, brand preferences, and so on.

Further empirical work allowed Bourne to attach 'valencies' to the brands of certain products and to product groups themselves denoting high or low reference group influence. Four possibilities exist: strong product valency with either strong or weak brand valency, and weak product valency with either strong or weak brand valency.

Table 6.1 shows the products which Bourne allocated to each of these four categories.

Table 6.1 : Reference Group Influence

Product Valency		Brand Valency		Examples
Strong	(+)	Strong	(+)	cars, cigarettes, beer, drugs.
Strong	(+)	Weak	(−)	Air conditioners, instant coffee, black and white TV.
Weak	(−)	Strong	(+)	Clothing, furniture, magazines, refrigerator (type), toilet soap.
Weak	(−)	Weak	(−)	Soap, canned peaches, laundry soap, refrigerator (brand), radios.

Source: Derived from Foundation for Research on Human Behaviour. *Group Influence in Marketing and Public Relations*, FRHB, 1956, p. 8.

Socially distant reference groups include footballers and filmstars who are often employed in advertisements on the assumption that they constitute positive reference groups for large sections of the audience. Despite this, however, comparatively little is known about the power to influence a consumer which is possessed by 'a group to which he is attracted, but with which he has little or no interaction'. This is how the term socially distant reference group is defined by Cocanougher and Bruce [16] who investigated the phenomenon among Texan college students. The reference group involved was businessmen. The authors report significant evidence for the usefulness of this concept in marketing and suggest that it may be possible to use consumers' attraction towards socially distant reference groups as the criterion for formulating market segmentation policies.

The notion of negative reference groups is also relevant here. These are groups or individuals whose behaviour, beliefs, values and so on, an individual deliberately avoids adopting as his own. It is probable that consumers select reference groups which are compatible with their self-images and ideal self-images and that the use of inconsistent distant others in advertisements will elicit a positive response only in consumers who have already adopted the appropriate groups as personal reference points. Any distant reference group is bound to affect some segment of the market in this way and care must be taken to measure the possible extent of this before marketing plans are operationalised.

Interpersonal Communication

An intriguing and influential theory about the role that is played by groups in the communications process arose from Lazarsfeld's studies of the 1940 U.S. Presidential election. [17] The fears of many intellectuals that the mass media were unduly influential in moulding public opinion were shaken by the finding that virtually no voters in that election appeared to have been influenced through formal channels of communication. It became apparent from empirical investigations of the process of mass communication that 'people come to the media, as to other messages, seeking what they want, not what the media intend them to have' and further that, as people have considerable choice between the media's offerings and because people are distant from the sources of messages reaching them through the media, they rely greatly on their social groups for a context within which to interpret messages received via the formal communications system. [18]

The Two-step Flow Hypothesis

Recognition of these facts led to the formulation of the two-step flow of communication hypothesis which postulates that the effects of mass media communications are not felt directly by the majority of the people. Rather, messages from the mass media are picked up by a relatively few influential individuals (called opinion leaders) who, in turn, disseminate information to the non-leader members of their informal social groups by means of word-of-mouth or interpersonal communication.

In what has now become a famous quotation, the authors of this theory, Lazarsfeld, Berelson and Gaudet, sum up its basic implications thus: '........ideas often flow from radio and print to the opinion leaders and from them to the less active sections of the population. [19]

Evidence has been accumulated in support of the belief that informal or word-of-mouth communications may be more influential than formal or mass communication and for the existence of opinion leaders who appear to share certain social and attitudinal characteristics. Interpersonal communication has been found by Katz and Lazarsfeld to be several times more effective than advertising in influencing housewives to select different brands of household products, [20] while Beal and Rogers report that informal sources of information can be much more effective than formal channels in persuading housewives to try new fabrics such as Nylon and Dacron. [21]   In a study of advertising relating to a new supermarket, Atkin found that, while eighty per cent of women exposed to word-of-mouth advertising actually tried the new shop, only forty-eight per cent of those exposed to formal advertising did so. [22]

Opinion Leaders

Some controversy surrounds the concept of opinion leadership, especially with reference to its usefulness in marketing management. Before considering the problems involved in the term's usage, it will be of value to consider the evidence for the existence of persons who adopt the role of opinion leader.

Katz and Lazarsfeld's exploratory studies [23] identified the following characteristics of the opinion leaders in four areas cognate to marketing. [24]

Food Purchasing
the opinion leader was a married woman with a rather large family, and an extroverted personality.

Fashion
the opinion leader was 'young and highly gregarious' and of a rather higher status.

Public Affairs
the opinion leader was of a high status, sociable and gregarious; there was a tendency for her influence to transcend status groups but always in the sense that she would mould the opinion of those of lower status.

Cinema-going

the opinion leader was usually a single young woman.

Table 6.2 : Correlates of Opinion Leadership

Variable	*Characteristics of Opinion Leaders*
Demographic and Social	Slightly higher social status than non-leaders may be apparent but some tendency towards homogeneity in age, income and also status.
	Extremely sociable and gregarious; great participation in wide range of social affairs.
	'Cosmopolitan' interests and interaction extend beyond local community.
Innovativeness	Tend to be innovative; positive response to new products both generally and within their own sphere(s) of interest and influence.
Psychographics	Equivocal evidence; some researchers have found no relationship between opinion leadership and a wide range of personality traits; others report that opinion leaders for women's fashions are assertive, stable, confident, self-esteeming. Confidence seems to be a general attribute, too.
Self-image	Perceive themselves as more interested in the area for which they are opinion leaders than do non-leaders.
Life-style	More exposure to mass media both generally and for specific area(s) of interest. Also more interpersonal communication with other consumers and other opinion leaders.
Conformity	Some evidence that opinion leaders adhere strictly to the norms of their social groups. This in itself contributes to their slightly enhanced social status within the group.

Sources: Derived from J.F. Engel *et al.*, *Consumer Behaviour*, Holt, Rinehart and Winston, 1973; E.M. Rogers and F.F. Shoemaker, *Communication of Innovations*, Free Press, 1971.

The further general characteristics of opinion leaders have been investigated by many researchers and their findings are summarised in Table 6.2. The generalisations included in that table reflect a good deal of subjectivity and cannot be taken as the final characteristics of opinion leaders in the absence of considerable further empirical data.

Innovativeness and Opinion Leadership

While opinion leadership is only one of several correlates of innovativeness in consumers (see Table 6.3 which indicates the variables for which on balance the research evidence suggests positive or negative correlations)

Table 6.3 : Correlates of Innovativeness

Variable Group	*Characteristics*
Consumer Variables	(Positively correlated:) education, literacy, standard of living, age, knowledgeability, attitude to change, achievement motivation, aspirations for children, business orientation, empathy.
	(Negatively correlated:) satisfaction with life, mental rigidity.
Product Variables	(Positively correlated:) relative advantage, compatability, need fulfilment, observability, availability, immediacy of benefit.
	(Negatively correlated:) complexity.
Social and Communication Variables	'Cosmopolitanness', exposure to mass media, contact with forces of change, deviancy, group participation, exposure to interpersonal communication, opinion leadership (all positively related).

Sources: Derived from J.F. Engel *et al.*, *Consumer Behaviour*, Holt, Rinehart and Winston, 1973; E.M. Rogers and J.D. Stanfield, 'Adoption and diffusion of new products', *Proc. American Marketing Association*. 1966.

it clearly has much in common with the tendency to try new products. Several of the factors listed in Table 6.2 as correlates of innovativeness also correlate highly with opinion leadership itself and many opinion leaders are to be found in the approximately two-and-a-half per cent of the population designated innovators by Rogers. [25]   (See Figure 6.3)

The relationship between opinion leadership, innovativeness and the two-step flow theory is highlighted by a study reported by Arndt [26] which monitored the diffusion of a new food product among four hundred and forty-nine housewives living in an aprtment complex. A letter informing housewives fo the availability of the new product was sent to each of the four hundred and ninety-five homes in the complex together with a coupon which reduced the price of the product to one third of its normal cost. Arndt gathered information about the sales of the product in the complex's store over a sixteen-day period of test; data were collected with respect to three variables at a subsequent interview. The subject's *adopter category* (see Figure 6.4) was ascertained from the pattern of coupon redemptions at the store. *Opinion leadership* was measured using sociometric techniques, respondents being asked the following question : 'When you want information about new food products you have not tried yet, are there any persons you would be particularly likely to discuss the new products with?' *Word-of-mouth behaviour* was determined by asking respondents

Figure 6.3 : The Diffusion Process

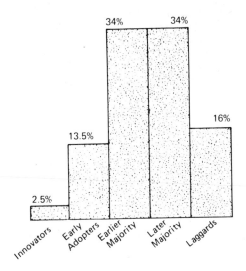

Source: E.M. Rodgers, *Diffusion of Innovations,* Free Press, 1962.

about comments they had made or received about the product; where possible questionnaires were checked against each other to cross-check the reliability of this information.

The results of the survey indicate:

1. that opinion leaders tended to be more influenced by formal communication than were the non-leaders;
2. that the opinion leaders had a tendency to be more active in communication both as transmitters and receivers;
3. that a great deal of information flowed from non-leaders to opinion leaders by means of word-of-mouth communcations;
4. that favourable word-of-mouth communications resulted in three times as many sales as unfavourable comments.

Apart from the emphasis on information flowing from non-leaders to opinion leaders, the results are completely in accord with the conclusions suggested by the two-step flow of communication theory. Nevertheless, that theory is not entirely satisfactory as an explanation of the communications networks of which consumers are a part.

Figure 6.4 : Adopter Categories

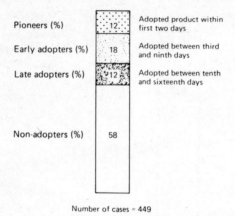

Pioneers (%) — 12 — Adopted product within first two days

Early adopters (%) — 18 — Adopted between third and ninth days

Late adopters (%) — 12 — Adopted between tenth and sixteenth days

Non-adopters (%) — 58

Number of cases = 449

Source: J. Arndt, 'A Test of the two-step flow in diffusion of a new product', *Journalism Quarterly*, 45, 1968.

Multi-phase Communication

The theory of the two-step flow of communication was once hailed as a breakthrough in our understanding of the process of mass communication and its effects on audiences. Nevertheless, despite the empirical evidence in its favour, it is now generally seen as no more than a rudimentary account of the way in which mass communications are received directly and indirectly. Its shortcomings have been pointed out by several writers and can be attributed in large part to the assumptions on which the basic two-step hypothesis was orginally based. In particular, it has been criticised in view of (a) the empirical finding that there is considerable communication between opinion leaders and other influencers and that much information passes from the so-called passive audience to opinion leaders; (b) its insistence that the audience is, for the most part, passive and does not seek out information actively; (c) the idea that formal and informal channels of communication are necessarily in competition one with the other; and (d) the finding that the formal channels of communication may have a more pervasive influence than was originally thought.

Goeke [27] has undertaken empirical research into the validity of the two-step idea and has argued that, while the theory assumes that opinion leaders are more likely to be exposed to relevant mass media than the people they influence, in practice the pervasiveness of the mass media leaves little room for interpersonal communication. He also concludes from his work that changes in voting behaviour among people with low political interest and low initiative can occur as a result of media influences as well as interpersonal influence.

The assumption that the audience is generally passive and inactive has been challenged by Cox [28] who has also put forward an alternative theory of communication. This assumes that the audience is actively seeking information about products and services on the market and that in so doing it uses three types of information channel in some form of optimal balance. The three sources are (1) manufacturer-dominated channels (the mass media and those elements of the marketing mix which the marketer controls); (2) consumer-dominated channels (word-of-mouth communications such as between friends, neighbours, relatives); and (3) neutral channels such as *Which?*, *Consumer Reports*, and editorial matter in magazines and newspapers which attempts to evaluate products.

Each of the three channels has its advantages and disadvantages for the potential buyer — the first is cheap but biased, the second is more objective but may not be readily available, the third is trustworthy but expensive — who is assumed to satisfy his need for information by which to evaluate product offerings by using all three in a complementary fashion. Marketing executives may thus stimulate informal information sources such as salesmen in retail outlets (who are assumed to have no loyalty to a particular manufacturer) to reinforce the messages carried by the formal channels. Public relations efforts may also be stepped up in order that the firm's image is not likely to detract from its advertising claims through interpersonal communications being critical of, say, the organisation's after-sales practices. Thus the Cox theory places much emphasis on the complementary interaction of the various sources of communication as well as on the information seeking of customers, and in both of these it is at odds with the two-step flow theory.

Perhaps the most important development of the two-step theory, however, is the more recent belief that communication is a multi-phase process. In particular, evidence points to the fact that opinion leaders communicate with other opinion leaders and obtain information from other influencing agents rather than simply from the mass media direct. Further, many non-leaders have been found to transmit information as well as receive it. [29] Engel *et al.* suggest that the idea of a chain of personal influence may characterise the communications process better than does the two-step picture. Figure 6.5 portrays a possible formulation of a multi-phase model of communication.

Figure 6.5 : Multi-phase Communication

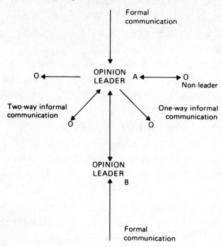

Social Influence and Situational Variables

One of the areas in which it has been suggested that research might be
carried out concerns the situational cues which trigger interpersonal
communication. [30] This introduces two related themes in recent
investigations, namely the social influence approach of King [31] and the
situational variables approach which has been propogated by Belk. [32]

Social influence in this sense refers to 'change or deviation from
expectation that results from other people's behaviour ....[it is] the
process by which the behaviour of one individual or collection of
individuals induces changes in the state of another individual or
collection of individuals'. [33] Social influence is evidently related to a
number of constructs which are widely employed in the behavioural
sciences and marketing — it cannot take place in the absence of persuasion
and communication and it often involves conflict resolution.

King advances the idea that there are five sources of social influence:
cultural factors, biological factors, psychological factors, social factors
and situational factors. Social and situational factors are especially
relevant to marketing for they include many of the factors already
discussed in this book. Social factors involve any relationship between
two or more people: trust, leadership, power status, role, reference
group, etc., while situational factors incude time, location, purpose,
participants, behaviour, message and so on. Social influence may have
three effects on individuals and groups. First, it can result in cognitive
changes (that is, changes in beliefs, knowledge, conceptions of the world,

especially of the actor's social world). Secondly, it may result in psychological changes (changes in motives, values and attitudes). And thirdly, it may manifest itself in behavioural changes (modifications to overt action). Marketing executives are interested in promoting all three types of change in their potential customers.

Social influence is of two types: normative (where the influencer intends to change the attitudes or behaviour of his audience) and informational (where the receiver is influenced in a manner not intended by the source). Most of the time in marketing situations, it is normative social influence with which executives are concerned but they need to be ever-aware of the effects of informational influence that is detrimental to the firm's profit and sales goals. For example, in the case of a new brand with a small market share, potential buyers are likely to take positive informational cues from users of older brands simply because those brands are better established. Advertising planning should take this into full consideration when the information load of messages is being determined.

Social Situations and Buying Behaviour

Situational factors have been taken into consideration in very few investigations of consumer behaviour but they appear to overcome some of the problems of the approach which look solely at social behaviour. The situational variables used by Belk include the consumer's physical surroundings, his social surroundings, his temporal perspective, his task definitions, and his antecedent states (e.g. depression or illness). [34]

While little additional research has been conducted along these lines, there are data on consumers' preferences for bread products showing that these vary considerably from one meal situation to another; and data showing that the choice of hairdryer types and brands can be related to characteristics of the receipient, and that information sources selected by buyers of tableware vary depending on whether the purchaser intends using the item himself or giving it as a present. Much of this may appear trite or simplistic but, to give a single example of its possible application, the information could assist greatly in decision making about the placing of advertisements. Furthermore, if the methodology which has already been used were applied to the resolution of other issues in consumer research (such as the one relating to the communications process posed at the beginning of this section) it might prove to be capable of eliciting more conclusive knowledge.

Applications

This chapter has covered a range of topics, some of which may appear to have limited relevance to marketing practice. But the use of group phenomena in marketing is very well established. Reference group effects and conformity are exploited generally but especially in advertising, and the 'slice of life' advertisements make use of a combination of factors including reference group influences and situational variables.

The marketing implications of the two-step theory have been briefly commented on above and those of the multi-phase model and Cox's account of communication which stresses the active search for information by consumers have also been mentioned. All of the contemporary theories of marketing communication make use of the notion of opinion leaders and this has resulted in some controversy. Useful as the term may appear, the identification of opinion leaders has proved difficult and expensive. Rogers has succeeded in isolating opinion leaders among farmers and another study has shown that innovative physicians who share many of the characteristics of 'influentials' can be identified (for instance, they have reference groups outisde their immediate locality, are younger than average for their professional group and tend to work with other doctors). [35]   Still it has not proved possible to find opinion leaders for many products and services to communicate with and influence them in an effective manner — if opinion leaders, by definition, are those who are influenced by the mass media, it is difficult to discover and exploit new methods of influencing them or of reducing the costs involved in advertising via the mass media. Thus, except in the case of some professional groups who can be contacted by salesmen or at conferences, the notion of opinion leaders has not proved easy to use in practice. However, some sociometric and questionnaire techniques show some promise of at least identifying opinion leaders in a more satisfactory manner than has been possible hitherto. [36]

Another problem connected with this concept is the question of whether opinion leadership is specific to one product or a few cognate products or whether it is general. [37] There is mounting evidence that it has general relevance and a survey by King and Summers has demonstrated that there is considerable overlap among some product categories of opinion leader influence (the product areas are: food, fashions, detergents and other cleaners, cosmetics, household appliances, both large and small, and personal care items). The greatest amounts of overlap were found to exist between products closely related to each other. While several other studies confirm these results, there is still a need for more testing of the social and cultural conditions which accompany opinion leadership and identification of the product areas for which this factor may be specific. [38]

Despite these problems and the need to know much more about the ways in which consumers are influenced and the dispersion of innovative products, the areas of group processes and interpersonal communication is a fruitful one for marketing practice and shows signs of becoming increasingly relevant to consumer product development.

Summary

Groups are specifically defined in behavioural science to refer to collections of individuals brought together to achieve a particular purpose. Primary groups are characterised by face-to-face interaction and evolve norms which influence the behaviour of their members. Reference groups are social artifacts which the individual uses for purposes of comparison, aspiration and to obtain values and perspectives. Group membership usually imposes a degree of conformity on the person.

Consumers are vitally influenced by their group memberships and by their reference groups. Brand choice, conformity and independence depend to an extent on group affiliations, and reference group influences vary from product to product and brand to brand. Socially distant reference groups also have relevance for marketing but some segments of the population must be expected to regard them as negative reference points.

Theories of communication emphasise the place of informal groups in the dissemination of informational and persuasive messages. The two-step flow hypothesis assumes that messages flow from the mass media to opinion leaders and from them to less active members of the population. There is evidence that interpersonal communication is important in influencing consumers but this is not necessarily in competition with formal channels. Multi-phase communication is indicated by the facts that influential persons tend to communicate with with each other a great deal and that the supposed less active sections of the market communicate a lot with opinion leaders.

Opinion leaders can be identified but this usually involves a great deal of trouble and expense and there usually appear to be no easy means of communicating with them except through the mass media. Innovation has been associated with opinion leadership. Recent evidence gives the impression that opinion leadership is general rather than specific. The applications of group effects and interpersonal communication are considerable and a new approach based on identifying social and situational factors looks promising for further applied research.

Notes

1.   W.J.H. Sprott, *Human Groups*, Penguin Books, 1958, p. 9.
2.   H.H. Kassarjian and T.S. Robertson, *Perspectives in Consumer Behaviour*, Scott Foresman, 1973, p. 292.
3.   G.C. Homans, *The Human Group*, Routledge and Kegan Paul, 1951, p. 1.
4.   Kotler, for example, states that membership groups cannot be reference groups; see P. Kotler, 'Behavioural models for analysing buyers', *Journal of Marketing Research*, 29, 1965.
5.   T. Shibutani, 'Reference groups as perspectives', *American Journal of Sociology*, 60, 1955. It is worth noting that this author argues for the restriction of the term reference group to its third meaning.
6.   S. Asch, 'Opinions and social pressure', *Scientific American*, November 1955; see also, 'Effects of group pressure upon the modification and distortion of judgements', in Kassarjian and Robertson, *Perspectives in Consumer Behaviour*.
7.   S. Milgram, *Obedience and Authority: An Experimental View*, Tavistock, 1974.
8.   M. Argyle, *Social Interaction*, Methuen, 1969, p. 220.
9.   J.L. Moreno, *Who Shall Survive?*, Beacon House, 1953.
10.   See Argyle, *Social Interaction*, p. 237.
11.   Ibid., pp. 230ff.
12.   J.E. Stafford, 'Effects of group influences on consumer brand preferences', *Journal of Marketing Research*, 3, 1966.
13.   M. Venkatesan, 'Consumer behaviour: conformity and independence', *Journal of Marketing Research*, 3, 1966. (For further information on the theory of reactance see: J.W. Brehm, 'A theory of psychological reactance', unpublished paper, Duke University, 1965.)
14.   Ibid.
15.   Foundation for Research on Human Behaviour, *Group Influences in Marketing and Public Relations*, FRHB, 1956.
16.   A.B. Cocanougher and G.D. Bruce, 'Socially-distant reference groups and consumer aspirations', *Journal of Marketing Research*, 8, 1971.
17.   P.F. Lazarsfeld *et al.*, *The People's Choice*, Duell, Sloan and Pearce, 1944.
18.   E.W. Schram and D.F. Roberts, *The Process and Effects of Mass Communication*, University of Illinois Press, 1971, p. 51.
19.   Lazarsfeld *et al.*, *The People's Choice*, p. 151.
20.   E. Katz and P.F. Lazarsfeld, *Personal Influence*, Free Press, 1955.
21.   G.M. Beal and E. Rogers, 'Informal sources in the adoption process of new fabrics', *Journal of Home Economics*, October 1951.
22.   K.L. Atkins, 'Advertising and store patronage', *Journal of Advertising Research*, December 1962.
23.   Katz and Lazarsfeld, *Personal Influence*.
24.   Kassarjian and Robertson, *Perspectives in Consumer Behaviour*, p. 294.
25.   E.M. Rogers, *Diffusion of Innovations*, Free Press, 1962.

26.   J. Arndt, 'A test of the two-step flow in diffusion of a new product', *Journalism Quarterly*, 45, 1968.

27.   J.R. Goeke, 'Two-step flow of communication: the theory reexamined', *Proc. Sixteenth Annual Conference on Public Opinion Research of the American Association for Public Opinion Research*, 1961.

28.   D. Cox, 'The audience as communicators', in *Toward Scientific Marketing*, American Marketing Association, 1963.

29.   Engel, *Consumer Behaviour*, p. 403.

30.   Ibid.

31.   S.W. King, *Communication and Social Influence*, Addison-Wesley, 1975.

32.   R.W. Belk, 'Situational variables and consumer behaviour', *Journal of Consumer Research*, 2, 2, 1975.

33.   King, *Communication and Social Influence*, p. 6.

34.   Belk, 'Situational variables'.

35.   J.S. Coleman *et al.*, *Medical Innovation: A Diffusion Study*, Bobbs-Merrill, 1966.

36.   C.W. King and J.O. Summers, 'Overlap of opinion leadership across consumer product categories', *Journal of Marketing Research*, 7, 1970.

37.   G.R. Foxall, 'Industrial marketing: the role of opinion leaders', *Proc. Marketing Education Group Conference*, 1979.

38.   D.F. Midgley, *Innovation and New Product Development*, Croom Helm, 1977.

7 THE FAMILY AND CONSUMER SOCIALISATION

Many of the decisions made by consumers are taken within the environment of the family and are thus affected by the desires and attitudes of other family members. Many products are purchased on behalf of other members of the buyer's household, perhaps as gifts, and these purchases inevitably reflect some degree of joint decision making. Even the most personal of purchases can be influenced in some details by the behaviour of the buyer's family and this social group demands special attention from the consumer researcher.

During the last two centuries, the major economic function of the nuclear family has shifted from production to consumption and so any study of consumption behaviour is bound to involve the dynamics of this social institution. The centrality of the family in behavioural science for marketing echoes its importance in sociology generally. For, while some authorities have forecast the imminent demise of the family in Western societies, [1] others have noted the institution's stability and endurance. [2]

The family is vital because of its mediating function. It links the individual with a wider society and it is through this that the individual learns the roles appropriate to adult life. As a result, 'it is through the family that society is able to elicit from the individual his necessary contribution', [3] and that contribution is closely bound up with buying behaviour.

Family Forms and the Family Cycle

The most familiar form of the family in industrial societies is the *nuclear* or two-generational family which consists usually of a mother, father and their children. This is not to say that the *extended* family, which spans at least three generations, has entirely disappeared or is unimportant. Recent empirical studies of the family [4] have demonstrated the influence of extended kin (e.g. grandparents, uncles) on the overall family's behaviour and decisions. It is extremely useful, however, to concentrate our discussion on the nuclear form of the family because of its predominance. Some behavioural scientists also distinguish the *family of orientation* or *origin* (into which one is born) from the *family of procreation* or *marriage* (which one founds). Other forms of the family, those which arise from polygamous marriage, or communal living, are of such small significance in contemporary marketing that we can safely ignore them.

Families can also be classified according to the stage in the family life cycle they have reached. Thus Rosser and Harris [5] have spoken of *the home-making phase* (from marriage to the birth of the first child), *the procreation phase* (from the birth of the first child to the marriage of the first child), *the dispersion phase* (from the marriage of the first child to the marriage of the last) and *the final phase* (from the marriage of the last child to the death of the original partners).

This classification is of limited value to consumer researchers who require one more closely related to the economic circumstances of the family. Perhaps the most useful approach is a classification based on the ages of children; since children's needs vary greatly with age, many facets of the family's consumption behaviour are explained by this variable. In this respect, an appropriate framework for consumer behaviour research [6] is one that involves five stages which are distinguidhes by the age of the household head and the presence and ages of children (see Table 7.1).

Table 7.1 : Family Life Cycle

Phase	Age and Status of Household Head	Children
I	Single or married, under 40	None
II	Married, under 40	Young
III	Married, under 40	Older (none young)
IV	Married, 40 or over	All over 20
V	(Possibly alone) over 40	None

It is clear that each of these stages has its own implications for consumers' income and expenditure patterns. Family needs and the ability to satisfy them can be uniquely associated with each life cycle phase; consider, for example, the family's differential needs over time for furniture, baby clothes, school uniforms, food, cars and holidays. While it would be superfluous to specify here all the possible relationships between buying patterns and the life cycle, it is interesting to note one aspect of shopping which is closely associated with this variable, namely shopping frequency.

In a survey of fashion-buying behaviour undertaken in Cleveland (U.S.A.), Rich and Jain [7] report that there is a tendency for younger women to shop more frequently than older ones. Such a pattern is consistent with the expectation that younger women are likely to be more fashion-conscious than older women. It cannot be assumed, however, that this pattern holds true for all products. A study of buying behaviour involving grocery purchases made in the Newcastle upon Tyne area (U.K.) [8] leads to the conclusion that in this case women over 40 have a tendency to shop more frequently than younger housewives.

Furthermore, while Rich and Jain reported that 'the presence of children did not make any significance' to the fashion-related shopping of women of all ages, the Newcastle data indicate that the presence of children in the family is associated with an increased frequency of shopping trips regardless of the age of the housewife.

Once again, the results of the survey are in accordance with expectations about the nature of shopping trips for the product area involved. Table 7.2 shows the relevance of the family life cycle as a variable in consumer choice behaviour for a specific consumer product, dentifrice, where there appears to be scope for segmenting the marketing on the basis of usage rates, using household size, presence of children and the working status of the housewife.

Table 7.2 : Dentifrice Purchasers (by Life Cycle)

	All Buyers %	Heavy Buyers %
Household Size		
1 or 2	30	3
3	25	24
4	26	37
5 or more	19	31
With/Without Children		
With	53	66
Without	47	34
Working Status of Housewife		
Full time	20	19
Part time	27	33
Not working	53	48

Source: Derived from 'Audit', AGB Ltd, 1972.

Roles and Decision Making in the Family

As some of the traditional functions of the family have declined, others have taken on increased significance. Consumption planning has become a central function of the modern family in industrial societies and the different purchasing roles of various family members have become more important. Whiteside [9] has given an account of the socialisation of women into the family's major purchasing role and of the conflict that may arise as a result of their being not simply an agent for others (as wives and mothers often are) but also responsible for their own needs which have to be satisfied through the same monetary funds.

This depiction of the housewife as the 'family purchasing agent' is echoed and reinforced, albeit with critical intentions, by Galbraith's more recent terminology which characterises her as the family's 'consumption administrator'. [10]

While such phrases serve to stress the closeness of most housewives to the final act of purchase, they cannot be taken as a complete guide to the processes of decision making within the family or to the role behaviours which impinge on them. It is patently obvious that most housewives do not decide upon and plan all household consumption and that they are not responsible for all shopping activities. A variety of role players both within and external to the family affect purchase decision making. Thus Kotler [11] distinguishes five buying roles which must be taken into account in analyses of family buying behaviour. These are the *initiator* (the person from whom the idea of buying a certain product first comes), the *influencer* (who consciously or unconsciously affects the purchase in some way, perhaps as an opinion leader), the *decider* (who makes any of the decisions or sub-decision which determine the precise nature of the purchase), the *purchaser* (who actually carries out the final purchase) and the *user* (who makes practical use of the item bought). These roles will be seen to fit closely with the description of the buying process given in Chapter 1 as each has a particularly conspicuous emphasis at one or other of the stages involved.

Almost all family decisions are affected by more than one of these consumer roles. For example, the selection of a venue for a family trip, although paid for and purchased by the parents, may be initiated and strongly influenced by children. Again, the majority of men's toiletry products were, until recently, purchased by women (many still are), and firms had the possibility of influencing not only the user but the decider and purchaser to choose their brands. Persuading users alone, as common sense suggests, would hardly have resulted in maximised sales.

Husband-Wife Decision Making

A considerable amount of empirical consumer research has concerned the role behaviour of family decision units and, within this research, the theme of husband-wife interaction in the decision-making process has predominated. Several methodological difficulties are evident in the work that has been reported and a pervading problem is that of ensuring that both spouses are interviewed and that the interviews with spouses are carried out in a similar manner with each. The consequence of not ensuring this is that results,and therefore conclusions, are based on a single partner's perceptions of the decision situation and this can be highly biased. Davis, [12] for instance, claims that some of the differences in researchers' conceptualisations of husband-wife decision processes can be attributed to differences in sample composition from one survey to another.

Another factor which is bound to alter the way in which results are interpreted and research projects are designed is the change which is occurring in the general role structure and decision-making processes of the nuclear family in industrial societies. So before considering the empirical findings with respect to consumer behaviour in any detail, it may be worth examining briefly some of the conclusions of sociologists who have been active in this area.

Edgell, [13] for instance, in an investigation of 'spiralists' — those middle class workers whose career patterns show extensive and rapid advance advancement and who are geographically very mobile — reports that the role relationships of husbands and wives are closely associated with the husband's attitudes towards career success. When he attaches relatively great importance to this, his central interest in life is usually work and family roles are sharply dichotomised or segregated. Husbands and wives have their own spheres within the home and there is little overlap in their role relations. Relationships within the family are generally dominated by the husband. If the husband's job orientation is less engrossing, he is usually more interested in his home than his work, he shares roles with his wife to a greater extent and his relationships with other members of the family are egalitarian. Thus the husband's orientation to work has been identified as a factor which affects relationships throughout the family and which is potentially significant as a determinant of consumption behaviour within the family. These studies also serve to remind the consumer researcher that research results may not apply generally even to middle class families but that extraneous work variables may have a direct influence on domestic consumer decision processes.

Some generalisation is permissible, however, with regard to the changes taking place in family relationships. Young and Willmott, in their study of *The Symmetrical Family*, [14] report the emergence of what they call 'a new kind of family' which has three main characteristics'

1. the member's lives are centered primarily on the home;

2. the nuclear family counts for more than the extended family; and, most characteristically,
3. the roles of family members are much less segregated than in the past, i.e. there is not such a sharply defined division of labour within the home.

This emerging family structure is based on greater companionship between spouses and relationships within it are more egalitarian than has been the case in the past.

The chief implication of this for consumer researchers is the growing tendency for decisions taken within the family to be 'joint' that is, with both partners contributing to the decisions that are reached, increasingly, though not yet entirely, on an equal basis.

This has been borne out by consumer and social research undertaken before and after the Young and Willmott studies. Komarovsky[15] hypothesised that the amount of communication between husbands and wives varies directly with the egalitarianism and sharing of tasks displayed in the family. If one of the joint tasks is shopping, then the very scale and complexity of the operation demands considerable discussion between partners. Summarising the empirical evidence on husband-wife interaction which might help confirm or refute this hypothesis, Komarovsky concluded that :

1. there is a tendency for wives to have more influence in decision making in the lower socio-economic groups (and this suggests that the symmetrical type of family is to be found more in the middle classes);
2. there appears to be a curvilinear relationship between the family's social class and the extent of joint involvement in its decision processes: both low - and high-income groups show low joint involvement whereas middle-income families tend to be high in joint decision making; and
3. joint involvement is greater among younger couples than among older ones.

Although the studies on which these conclusions are based were carried out in the United States of America, there is some evidence that broadly similar patterns of behaviour exist among British and European consumers.[16]   Nevertheless, it should be noted that several of the American studies apply to specific products or decision areas and, as has been pointed out, the results of such studies are not always capable of universal application.

The possibility that either husbands or wives may predominate in decisions relating to particular products is confirmed by a well-known investigation of husband-wife relationships carried out by Kenkel. [17] In his study, some fifty married couples, each containing a husband who was a full-time student, were asked to decide how they would spend a windfall of $300. It was stipulated that the money could not be saved or used for a purchase the couple had already agreed on. Taped recordings of the ensuing discussions were analysed with respect to these three factors :

1. the relative amount of talking done by each spouse;
2. spouses' relative contributions to the maintenance of harmony during discussions; and
3. their **relative** generation of ideas, suggestions, opinions, etc.

The products mentioned by the couples were classified into five separate categories as follows :

1.	Wife personal	e.g.	clothes, jewelry.
2.	Wife household	e.g.	washing machine, cocking utensils.
3.	Husband	e.g.	books, clothes, watch.
4.	Joint family	e.g.	furniture, TV, Car.
5.	Children	e.g.	toys, clothes.

In forty per cent of the cases, husbands and wives were found to contribute equally to the discussions in terms of the amount of talking each did. In forty-two per cent of cases, husbands talked more than their wives. When husbands predominated, more items which were husband (or children) specific were decided upon than when husbands and wives did approximately the same amount of talking. In the remaining cases, where wives out-talked their husbands, more wife-personal goods were decided upon but the husbands still 'received' more items than in the first two cases.

In some sixty per cent of cases, husbands contributed more ideas and suggestions that did wives and, when this occurrred, fewer items for children were decided upon but more for the family as a whole resulted than when wives predominated.

Seventy-two per cent of the time, wives contributed to the harmony and smooth running of the conversations by raising their husbands' status, being affectionate, laughing or joking, Only twenty per cent of husbands behaved in this way.

The fact that Kenkel's study was conducted among American students who were presented with a hypothetical situation to make sense of means that it is difficult to place very much confidence in the applicability of his results to consumers in general. Certainly further evidence should be produced before the conclusions are widely accepted. This work does, however, serve to emphasise that interaction between husbands and wives in consumption decision processes depends on the self-perceptions and roles of family members, that differences of emphasis in product choice reflects role behaviour, and that personality's being an intervening variable between social groups and individual consumer choices is a possibility worthy of further investigation. While the results must be qualified by the nature of the investigation, therefore, they do demonstrate with some force the importance of the behaviour with which they are concerned to the unravelling of the family's influence on buying activity.

Role Perceptions and Decision Making

The empirical work which relates family roles and consumer choices has usually been carried out in the absence of a general theoretical frame framework and, as a result, comparison of behavioural findings from several studies is difficult. An exception is found in the work of Davis and Rigaux [18] who analysed the influence exerted by husbands and wives at differing stages in the process of consumption planning and decision making. Their investigation was designed to determine whether there are differences in partners' roles at different stages of the decision-making process and how husbands and wives perceive their roles at each stage of the process.

Husbands and wives in seventy-three households in Belgium were asked to provide information on their decision making relative to twenty-five products and services. Each respondent was required to specify the person who had been dominant in making the overall decision with regard to each of the twenty-five areas; the husband's dominant influence was indicated by the figure 1, the wife's by 3, and joint decision making by 2. Decisions could then be classified in one of four ways for the families as a whole: *husband-dominant* (where the mean relative influence lies between 1 and 1.5); *wife-dominant* (2.5 to 3); *syncratic* and *autonomic* (between 1.5 and 2.5). The last two categories require further explanation. When more than half the families made a joint decision with respect to an item, the decision was classified as syncratic; when fewer than half the families made the decision jointly, it was classed as autonomic.

The twenty-five decision areas were classified as follows:

Husband-dominant
life insurance, other insurance.
Wife-dominant
cleaning products, kitchenware, child clothing, wife clothing, food, other furnishings.
Autonomic
cosmetics, non-prescription drugs, appliances, housing upkeep, husband clothing, alcoholic beverages, garden tools, saving objectives, forms of saving, car.
Syncratic
children's toys, living-room furniture, outside entertainment, vacation, school, housing, TV.

Having demonstrated that purchase decision can be classified in this way (including the results of other investigations) Davis and Rigaux turned to the question of the nature of husband wife interactions at three stages in the decision-making process. The selected stages are (i) problem recognition (called 'development and perception of a want or need' earlier in this book), (ii) search for information ('pre-purchase planning and decision making') and (iii) final decision ('the purchase act'). The accompanying table (Table 7.3) shows the marital roles appear to vary from phase to phase in the decision process but the differences are by no means large, and may not be statistically significant.

Table 7.3 : Marital Roles and Decision Process Phases

		Phase		
		i	*ii*	*iii*
Husband-dominant		2	3	2
Joint		17	15	18
Wife-dominant		6	7	5
	Totals	25	25	25

Source: After H.L. Davis and B.P. Rigaux, 'Perception of marital roles in decision processes', *Journal of Consumer Research*, 1, 1, 1974. (Autonomic and syncratic categories have been merged and presented as joint decisions.)

Interestingly some decisions show the same type of influence throughout the process of decision making. Table 7.4 indicates those areas where thid is so, and nearly two-thirds of decisions come into this category (of the twenty-five decisions, sixteen show unchanged patterns of influence over the decision period as a whole).

Table 7.4 : Unchanged Patterns of Influence

Pattern of Influence	Decision Areas Not Changing
Husband-dominant	Life insurance, other insurance.
Wife-dominant	Kitchenware, cleaning products, wife's clothes, children's clothes, food.
Syncratic	Housing, living-room furniture, children's toys, school, entertainement, vacation.
Autonomic	Garden tools, alcoholic beverages, non-prescription drugs.

Source: Data from Davis and Rigaux, op. cit.

Nine decisions did change, however, and some of the patterns of change are shown in Table 7.5.

Table 7.5 : Changing Patterns of Influence

	Phase		
	i	*ii*	*iii*
Housing upkeep	Autonomic	Autonomic	Syncratic
Household appliances	Autonomic	Autonomic	Syncratic
Husband's clothing	Autonomic	Autonomlc	Syncratlc
Saving Objectives	Autonomic	Autonomic	Syncratic
Forms of saving	Autonomic	Autonomic	Syncratic
Car	Autonomic	Husband-dominant	Syncratic

Source: Data from Davis and Rigaux, op. cit.

The final part of the investigation involved role consensus, the extent to which partners agreed on their relative contributions to decision making. Over the data as a whole, sixty-eight per cent of couples agreed about their roles; Davis and Rigaux report that there was a 'range around this mean figure from fifty-seven per cent to eighty-eight per cent'. Where couples did not agree in their perceptions of role behaviour, their bias can be attributed to either 'vanity' (the spouse overestimates his/her own contribution and influence and plays down those of the partner partner) or 'modesty' (the spouse underestimates his/her own contribution and gives undue emphasis to that of the partner). Vanity was especially evident as a source of bias, particularly in the second phase (information search). Although the aggregated data showed a fairly high level of agreement, the within-family role consensus was considerably smaller, though still higher than chance alone would allow. The implication of this for market researchers is that for general research it may be sufficient to interview only one spouse (usually this is the wife); but if the researcher wishes to classify individual families by role structure it remains necessary to interview both husbands and wives.

The Davis and Rigaux study is of considerable significance in consumer research. First, it provides a classification which should be useful in further investigations and which can accommodate the findings of some earlier studies. Secondly, it is of value for the market researcher and may bring to an end the controversy over the interviewing of one or both partner(s). Thirdly, it provides a valuable study which has been conducted outside the United States. Nevertheless, the study has some shortcomings, some of which are recognised and commented upon by the authors. The sample is small (seventy-three families) and was chosen by students on the basis of convenience and accessibility. The manner in which data were obtained is also suspect: husbands and wives were asked to give their impressions of who contributed what influence to the decision made, and, more difficult still, to assess the relative contributions of husband and wife at three separate stages in the decision process. These data are bound to be subjective and may even conceal deliberate falsehood if a respondent does not wish to admit to the extent of his or his partner's influence in general household decision making.

Other Approaches

Two other recent approaches to the study of husband-wife interaction in consumer decision amking deserve mention. An earlier survey reported by Davis [19] although superseded in some degree by that just described, produced some interesting results with respect to purchases of cars and furniture. It highlights the futility of asking general questions such as 'Do husbands or wives make the decision to buy a car? ' In the case of cars, husbands rather than wives decided when to buy the item in over two-thirds of cases, but in only one quarter of cases did the husband have more influence than the wife when it came to selecting the colour of the car. These figures happened to be the same whether the husband was asked for his perception of the buying process or whether the information came from the wife. However, in other matters, there were large differences in the roles played by husbands and wives according to their separate perceptions and Davis concluded that 'it would be misleading to generalise about husband and wife roles in any absolute sense'.

Considerable role consensus was also apparent. In the case of cars, an average sixty-three per cent of couples showed agreement about the roles they played while for furniture purchases the proportion was sixty-one per cent. Both figures come close to double the proportions which a chance distribution of roles alone would lead one to expect, namely one third. Again, Davis's work emphasises not merely the product about which a decision is being made but also the nature of the decision itself.

A quite distinct approach to this field is that of Ferber and Lee [20] who investigated the notion that families usually have one member responsible for finances for the family as a whole. They designated this person the Family Financial Officer (FFO) and examined his/her behaviour with respect to three aspects of domestic spending:

(a) Looking after the payment of bills.
(b) Keeping track of expenditure in relation to budgets.
(c) Use of money left over at the end of the pay period.

Their work focused on newly married young couples and was extremely valuable in that data were gathered at six-monthly intervals over several years.

It was found comparatively easy to identify an FFO in each family and if the three tasks specified for the person with this role were jointly carried out, the couple itself was designated the FFO. A spouse who looks after two of the three jobs was also designated the FFO. Two lots of information were presented in this paper, one gathered during the couples' first year of marriage, the other one a year later. Figure 7.1 depicts the changes which took place in this role between the two periods. It is clear that after an initial emphasis on joint decision making, the wife increasingly took over the FFO role.

However, identifying the FFO is one thing; making use of the concept in marketing is quite another. A means of bridging the gap involves elucidating the factors which determine whether husband or

Figure 7.1 : The Family Financial Officer (FFO)

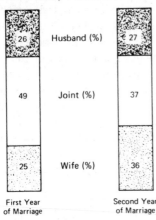

Source: R.F. Ferber and L.C. Lee, 'Husband-wife influence in family purchasing behaviour', *Journal of Consumer Research*, 1, 1, 1974.

wife becomes the FFO or whether the role is carried out jointly. Ferber and Lee state that, when the role was played by a single individual, there was a great tendency for the wife to assume the responsibility if she was 'more quality-minded, more economy-minded, or more bargain-minded'. This was the case in families where there was a likelihood of financial disagreements, too, especially where the disagreement involved saving priorities.

Couples were likely to act jointly where both spouses shared a savings goal and where their ideas about savings priorities coincided. When the husband took on the role of FFO, savings as a proportion of total income tended to be higher; and while car purchases tended to be less frequent in this case, durable purchases as a whole were not affected.

This study is useful for emphasising the fact that the family's economic behaviour is not always the result of unified or homogeneous planning and action and usually involves different role dimensions. Again, it lends support to the idea that for some purchase and saving decisions marketing and consumer researchers need to obtain accurate information from both partners instead of relying on one family member for all their data.

Children and the Socialisation Process

The influence of children on family expenditure has long been recognised and advertisers have frequently made use of this fact to persuade parents to buy certain products through appeals to their children. The market for children's products has itself grown rapidly in the last several decades and the teenage market in particular is a very attractive segment for many manufacturers and marketers.

Despite this, consumer behaviour specialists do not know a great deal about the way in which children are influenced or the process whereby young people learn the consumption roles which characterise adults. The area of consumer socialisation is a potentially fruitful one for marketing management yet, until recently, socialisation was a subject studies almost exclusively by social psychologists, sociologists and to a lesser extent polotical scientists. In view of the importance of the subject and the fact that our knowledge of the processes and structures involved in consumer socialisation is not advanced, it seems reasonable to approach the area by first offering a definition of consumer socialisation and, secondly, examining those aspects of the socialisation process which promise to be most fruitful as areas for future research.

Consumer Socialisation

Socialisation is generally understood by behavioural scientists to refer to the process in which individuals learn the roles and attitudes thought appropriate by society for their adult lives. There is thus a great emphasis in the social science literature on the socialisation of children and the effects of the various family members on this process. Goode, in the book cited earlier, defines socialisation as 'the process by which the young human being acquires the values and knowledge of his group and learns the social roles appropriate to his position in it'. But, while there is naturally an emphasis on child socialisation, this is a process which continues throughout life as the individual learns new roles and acquires new behaviour and attitudes. As will become clear in the following account, the process of socialisation has much in common with that of learning.

In the first major review of consumer socialisation, Scott Ward [21] defines this as the 'processes by which young people acquire skills, knowledge, and the attitudes relevant to their functioning as consumers in the marketplace', a definition which immediately narrows the framework of analysis of the consumer researcher to economic behaviour in the market-place.

Although it is generally acknowledged that socialisation is a useful and important concept for the social scientist, it might be argued that it is of questionable value in marketing. Why should we give our attention to the formation of consumer wants and needs rather than taking the final demand patterns of consumers as given? Ward provides several answers which are applicable to practitioners as well as academic researchers.

First, it might be possible to predict aspects of adult behaviour through understanding childhood experiences. The way in which the individual originally learns to process information gained from advertisements might well, for instance, affect his adult attitudes towards and responses to advertising. Indeed, much information about adult customers may be available to us *only* through an understanding of childhood behaviour and the formation of attitudes and beliefs in young people.

Secondly, knowing how young people acquire 'consumption-related skills, knowledge and attitudes' and isolating the factors that influence children should help ensure that marketing campaigns aimed at children become more effective. In the past, much advertising to children has been found on trial and error methods rather than precise knowledge of children's decision processes.

Thirdly, child socialisation may hold a key to the understanding of family decision making with respect to consumption. As we have seen, a great deal of research has concentrated on husband-wife interaction but relatively little has involved children. Knowing more about this facet of the process in which family decisions are made should help in the explanation and evaluation of the effects of one generation on another's behaviour.

Fourthly, Ward suggests that knowledge of child consumer socialisation might be useful to those people who formulate government policy with respect to consumer protection and to those responsible for consumer education, including home economists. In view of some of the apparently arbitrary decisions made by some consumer protection agencies, consumer protection legislation surely should be based more firmly on empirical behavioural science research findings on childhood reactions to marketing.

Fifthly and finally, there may be theoretical advantages in under understanding more fully the socialisation of children into adult consumer roles. Models of the consumer consumption process have not accentuated this aspect of consumer behaviour and it is possible that further research might enhance the predictive capabilities of such theoretical constructs. Nevertheless, many consumer researchers would argue that this is an optimistic hope and that much more basic research is required before sophisticated theories of consumer socialisation are likely to emerge.

Research Directions

The earliest studies of children and consumption stem from the work of classical and contemporary sociologists rather than being surveys of child buying in a marketing context. One of the first practical studies, however, was carried out by McNeal [22] in the mid-1960s and was addressed to the question: what factors influence children in their acquisition of consumer roles? We know that the influence of parents declines as the child grows older and it is also clear that family influences are, as a rule, more important than those of peer groups in early childhood. Nevertheless, several studies have shown that very little purposive consumer training takes place in most families and that parents often expect their children to learn from observation and to imitate the behaviour of other family members.

Although McNeal's study was essentially exploratory, it nevertheless provides some leads on these matters. It indicates, for instance, that children acquire a considerable amount of independence between the ages of five and nine and that parents generally expect their offspring to make more complex decisions on the basis of personal observation, judgement and experience as they grow older.

But what forces take over as parental influence wanes? What impact does advertising have on children's preferences? And what are the results of interpersonal communication, especially with peers?

Advertising appears to exert a considerable influence on children but it is not known how young people process or evaluate the claims made by advertisers or how they distinguish the persuasive elements of advertising from the purely informative aspects. Theories of cognitive development have been suggested as a source of constructs and ideas with which to investigate the information-processing mechanism of children as they learn their consumption-related roles but there is little empirical knowledge to justify this approach. The precise interrelationship of parental influences and formal communication is also unknown; perhaps formal and informal communication are paramount in determining brand choices while family factors and exposure to advertising account for child consumers' general materialistic orientations and attitudes. But as yet this remains an untested hypothesis, and little enough is known about the social meanings customers in general attach to material goods and the origin of these meanings.

Another area for research is what some social scientists have called 'reverse socialisation' — the process in which children influence their parents' roles. The range of products where children have the power to make and implement direct purchase decisions is restricted but young people can have a pervasive influence on household decision making with respect to such items as cars, holidays and even furniture. In contrast, Berey and Pollay [23] have demonstrated that mothers who are relatively child-centred show more concern for their children's welfare than is typical, do not give in to their youngsters' demands for particular types of cereal as often as do less child-centred mothers. Likewise, assertive children were not found to be more successful in engineering their mothers' behaviour to provide the cereals desired by the children than less assertive children.

A recent study by Ward and Wackman [24] was concerned with a range of products: foods (including breakfast cereal, snacks, sweets, soft drinks, bread, coffee and petfood), durables for children's own use (including toys, clothes, bicycles, record albums and cameras), toiletries (including toothpaste, bath soap, shampoo and aspirin) and other items including household cleaners and laundry soap. For most types of product, mothers were more likely to yield to children's demands as the children grew older though the authors point out that this might be because older children ask for less. But it could stem from the fact that parents believe that their children are more competent judges as they get older and are therefore more capable consumers to whom the mother should listen. The products mothers were most likely to give in about were food items and these were also the products children made most demands for. Over all, Ward and Wackman reported a correlation between children's influence attempts and parental yielding of 0.35 which in terms of the sample used was both positive and statistically significant. Although the relationship is not a particularly strong one, the study none the less provides clear evidence that the more children ask for products, the more they receive them – a finding which is not entirely consistent with the reported 'gatekeeper effect' apparent from Berey and Pollay's work. Replication of other people's research may sound dull but this is obviously an area which demands it.

A third area in which consumer researchers might take greater interest is that of adult consumer socialisation. Research could usefully be directed at investigating the transitions consumers make from one role to another and the implications for consumption attitudes and behaviour. Products bought directly by children are, for the most part, small and inexpensive items which are frequently repurchased. Adult consumers, while they do purchase things of this type, also buy large, expensive articles which are much more infrequently renewed. It would be interesting to know how the transition from one type of buying to the other takes place, the way in which self-perceptions change as consumers take on new roles and the information they seek as new consumer-related responsibilities are acquired.

We have seen that the traditional roles of men and women in industrial societies may be breaking down despite the relative stability of the family as a social institution (at the present time only approximately seven per cent of marriages in Britain end in divorce). [25] This 'role-blurring' and the sharing of responsibilities involved in the role of 'Family Financial Officer' have important consequences for the marketing manager who advertises to family groups and are direct results of new forms of socialisation.

Future research in the area of child consumer socialisation needs to be much more rigorous than previous work has been with respect to both survey design and data gathering. Small samples and big conclusions have characterised much of the work that has hitherto been carried out and there has been a tendency to avoid quantification. Asking children about their own past behaviour and expecting them to provide reliable information about parental influences is naive to say the least. In one survey, teachers' ideas of children's assertiveness were taken as reliable guides to their relationships with their parents even though assertiveness in the classroom may coexist in the same child with compliance at home.

Longitudinal research, requiring the observation of a series of events rather than taking 'snapshot' impressions of behaviour, is also called for. This may mean the use of more expensive and sophisticated methods of gaining information but is likely to yield more reliable and practical results.

Summary

The family is the context within which many consumer decisions are made and there is thus wide scope for the attitudes and behaviour of one family member to influence the purchase behaviour of another. The nuclear family is the predominant form of this institution in industrial society and seems fairly stable and enduring. Consumer need and the ability to satisfy them vary from stage to stage of the family life cycle: home making, procreation, dispersion and the last phase. Shopping behaviour for some products varies significantly with life cycle stage.

Patterns of husband-wife interaction in the consumption decision-making process are complex and there are severe methodological problems involved in discovering exactly who makes what decisions.

As a rule, it is impossible to find out who makes an overall decision but patterns of influence can be identified and responsibility for sub-decision sub-decisions allocated to either husband or wife. The roles of husbands and wives appear to vary from phase to phase of the decision-making process; specific products and decision areas can be classified as husband-dominant, wife-dominant, autonomic or syncratic. However, high levels of role consensus have been identified showing that husbands and wives tend to agree on who made what decisions and sub-decisions. For those types of decision where role consensus is high, marketing researchers need interview only one spouse. The notion of a Family Financial Officer (FFO) has some validity. FFOs can be identified quite easily and the attributes or circumstances which lead to one or other spouse being designated FFO have been isolated. Whether the husband or wife is FFO has special implications for the pattern of family spending and saving.

Consumer socialisation promises to throw considerable light on the consumption process but more basic research is required into the areas of role acquisition, reverse socialisation and adult consumer socialisation. More rigorous research techniques are called for.

Notes

1. D. Cooper, *The Death of the Family*, Penguin Books, 1976.
2. R. Fletcher, *The Family and Marriage in Britain*, Penguin Books, 1966.
3. W.J. Goode, *The Family*, Prentice-Hall, 1964, p. 3.
4. M. Young and P. Wilmott, *Family and Kinship in East London*, Routledge and Kegan Paul, 1957; *The Symmetrical Family*, Penguin Books, 1975.
5. C. Rosser and C.C. Harris, *The Family and Social Change*, Routledge and Kegan Paul, 1965.
6. See C.G. Walters, *Consumer Behaviour*, Irwin, 1974, p. 249.
7. S.U. Rich and S.C. Jain, 'Social class and life cycle as predictors of shopping behaviour', *Journal of Marketing Research*, 5, 1968.
8. G.R. Foxall, 'Social factors in consumer choice: replication and extension', *Journal of Consumer Research*, 2, 1, 1975.
9. H.O. Whiteside, 'Investigating the roles of the household purchasing agent', in R. Cox *et al.* (eds), *Theory in Marketing*, Irwin, 1964.
10. J.K. Galbraith, *Economics and the Public Purpose*, Penguin Books, 1976.
11. P. Kotler, *Marketing Management*, Prentice-Hall, 1972, p. 113.
12. H.L. Davis, 'Dimensions of marital roles in consumer decision-making', *Journal of Marketing Research*, 7, 1970.
13. S. Edgell, 'Spiralists: their careers and family lives', *British Journal of Sociology*, 40, 1970.
14. Young and Willmott, *The Symmetrical Family*, pp. 29-33.
15. M. Komarovsky, 'Class differences in family decision-making', in N.N. Foote (ed), *Household Decision-Making*, New York University Press, 1961.
16. Young and Willmott, *The Symmetrical Family*.

17.   W.F. Kenkel, 'Husband wife interaction in decision-making and decision choices', *Journal of Social Psychology*, 54, 1961.

18.   H.L. Davis and B.P. Rigaux. 'Perceptions of marital roles in decision processes', *Journal of Consumer Research*, 1, 1, 1974.

19.   Davis, 'Perceptions of marital roles'.

20.   R. Ferber and L.C. Lee, 'Husband wife influences in family purchasing behaviour', *Journal of Consumer Research*, 1, 1, 1974.

21.   S. Ward, 'Consumer socialisation', *Journal of Consumer Research*, 1, 2, 1974.

22.   J.U. McNeal, *An Exploratory Study of the Consumer Behaviour of Children*, University of Texas at Austin, 1964.

23.   L.A. Berey and R.W. Pollay, 'Influencing role of the child in family decision-making', *Journal of Marketing Research*, 5, 1968.

24.   S. Ward and D.B. Wackman, 'Children's purchase influence attempts and parental yielding', *Journal of Marketing Research*, 9, 1972.

25.   T. Johns, *Social Structure of Modern Britain*, Pergamon, 1973.

8 SOCIAL STRATIFICATION AND CONSUMER DECISION MAKING

Nearly everyone has some impression of a system of social classes and of their own position within that system. Most people would readily be able to say where they think various occupational groups — especially prominent ones such as doctors, teachers, miners — should be located in the class system and there is often wide agreement on this among all of the groups involved. Subjective impressions of class are confirmed by statistics which show that many of the social, economic, psychological and even physical characteristics of people vary significantly from one class to another. Some of the differences associated with the various social classes are : fertility rates, infant mortality rates, education, socialisation patterns, religion, divorce rates, income, the incidence and extent of certain diseases, mortality rates and occupation.

In a relatively open society, social class is not a determinant of behaviour in any absolute sense since there is scope for social mobility between classes and class is not the only criterion used in evaluating an individual's ability to perform tasks. This may be compared to the situation in a caste system where movement from one social position to another is extremely difficult, if not quite impossible.

The pervasiveness of class-related phenomena in any society extends, naturally enough, to consumer behaviour and is manifested not only in product and brand preferences and usage rates but in several other facets of consumer behaviour such as shopping frequency, store attitudes and susceptibility to advertising campaigns. For the manager, social class offers a convenient means of segmenting markets and even within the context of the increasingly popular life-style segmentation, social class plays an important role. Consumer researchers have long been interested in measuring social *class* and advertising men have also exploited the *status* differences between consumers. This chapter is concerned with both of these dimensions of social stratification and their effects on consumer decision making.

The Meaning of Social Class and Status

The fundamental reasoning behind the idea of social stratification is that society can be conceptualised as a series of divisions arranged so that some are above others in a hierarchy much the same as layers of rock are arranged in geological stratification. The notion of social stratification requires some refinement, however, since the divisions to which it refers are not discrete and the picture is constantly changing due to upward and downward social mobility. There are also several definitions of social stratification's three main elements or dimensions : class, status and power. We will focus our attention on the meanings attached to class and status, since, while power is an important factor in consumer decision making, it can usually be treated in connection with the broader influence of class.

Social Class

Much of the confusion which surrounds the concept of class derives from the imprecise way in which the term is used and its treatment as if it were synonymous with status. Often the phrase 'socio-economic status' is used in place of class but in this chapter the concepts of class and status are treated as separate, yet related elements of stratification. Another source of imprecision stems from the tendency to omit economic considerations from definitions of class even though it has been emphasised that occupation and (source of) income are major determinants of social class.[1]

What then is the best way to define social class? We may say that it refers to divisions in the population which are based on economic criteria such as occupation and income or wealth which determine to some extent the way of life of those belonging to each division. Definitions of such a wide-ranging phenomenon are bound to be arbitrary despite the fact that there is common agreement that all known societies are stratified in some way Cotgrove[2] states, for instance, that class 'refers to the existence of solidary groupings which arise on the basis of ..... differences in income, prestige and power'. And Berger[3] says that class is 'a type of stratification in which one's general position in society is basically determined by economic criteria'. Each of these definitions stresses the centrality of economic position to the idea of class and suggest that the variable of socio-economic class provides a useful framework for statements about social behaviour.

Some difficulty has arisen in operationalising the notion of class and in selecting suitable criteria or 'proxy variables' for measuring class in practical situations. For Marx and his followers the sole criterion is one's relationship to the means of production and Marx recognised two major classes, the bourgeoisie (who owned the factories, distribution systems, and so on) and the proletariat (who owned no more than their

ability to work the means of production); on the basis of this
dichotomy, Marx built an elaborate theory of social change and
revolution which included predictions of the growing enmiseration of
the working classes, polarisation of the bourgeoisie and proletariat, and
a violent overthrow of the former by the latter. Although his
predictions are generally accepted as being erroneous by many
sociologists, many still find his fundamental account of the
determinants of social class a useful one for their research. Consumer
researchers tend to find it inadequate since they desire a more flexible
division of society with more than two classes; they also require
divisions which are clearly related to consumption behaviour.

Another well-known social scientist, Max Weber, went beyond
Marx's classification and based his own system of class on the
ownership of property; this included both industrial and domestic
property.[4] While Weber's contribution has also been important to
sociology, it still lacks sufficient detail for the purposes of market
segmentation.

In most areas of consumer research, it is preferable to define class in
terms of a set of economically related variables for which national or
international statistics are available. These proxy variables include
income, source of income, occupational grouping and dwelling area.
While none of these is wholly indicative of social class, they represent
the most direct practical way of making the concept of class usable
in the real world of consumption and marketing. The manner in which
they can be made operational is discussed below.

Social Status

The second dimension of stratification which is of interest in consumer
research is that of status. Status refers to the honour or prestige which
society accords to the occupants of certain social positions. Again the
notion of hierarchy is relevant and, in Western societies at least, a
physician is normally given a higher status than, say, a road-sweeper;
if the physician is a general practitioner, however, his status may be
lower than that given to a brain surgeon. The prestige ratings of selected
occupations in the U.S.A. are shown in Table 8.1.

While status reflects economic factors, it does not necessarily
coincide with class. Impoverished aristocrats, to take an extreme
example, may well be accorded status which does not reflect their
current wealth but which is based on past wealth, behaviour, manners,
accent and other social criteria. Similarly, making a large amount of
money does not guarantee a high status unless one adopts other

Table 8.1 : Prestige Rankings of Occupations (U.S.A., 1963)

Occupation	Rank
U.S. Supreme Court Justice	1
Physician	2
Scientist	3.5
Lawyer	11
Dentist	14
Psychologist	17.5
Priest	21.5
Banker	24.5
Teacher	29.5
Novelist	34.5
Electrician	39
Policeman	47
Barber	62.5
Nightclub Singer	74
Farm Hand	83
Garbage Collector	88
Street Sweeper	89
Shoe Shiner	90

Sources: Derived from R.W. Hodge *et al.*, 'Occupational prestige in the United States, 1925-1963', in R. Bendix and S.M. Lipset (eds), *Class, Status and Power*, Free Press, 1966.

patterns of behaviour which command more prestige. It has been argued that in a class society where mobility is not only possible but a reality, there is a need to show others that one has been upwardly mobile, that one has 'arrived' and that this is done by means of status symbolism, 'by the use of various symbols (such as material objects, styles of demeanour, taste, and speech, types of association and even appropriate opinions)'.[5]

Status differentiations cut across social class but they are evidently related; Weber himself stated that 'with some over-simplification, one might thus say that "classes" are stratified according to their relations with the production and acquisition of goods; whereas "status groups" are stratified according to the principles of their consumption of goods as represented by special "styles of life".'[6]

Measurement of Socio-economic Class

Enough has been said about social class and consumer behaviour to make it clear that class is of little use in marketing research unless it can be measured in some consistent manner which helps in the prediction of buying behaviour. Generally, behavioural scientists are interested in social class as an objective phenomenon; that is, they employ criteria which place given individuals indisputably into one class or another no matter who carries out the analysis. It is sometimes useful, however, to know how consumers perceive themselves as far as class is concerned and, in any case, it is not a bad principle to provide a continuing check on the social relevance and meaning of objective measures.

Subjective Measures of Social Class

It is sometimes argued that class is no longer an important variable for describing differences in society. Brown[7] for example, has written: 'We shall argue that contemporary life in the United States is not stratified at all; that there are no classes here.' The reality of social class is apparent, however, not only from patterns of inequality which may be identified 'objectively' in all societies, but from individuals' subjective evaluations of class.

The Lynds,[8] in their classic study of 'Middletown', discovered that the majority of people in this typical American town were able to place occupational groups into a nine-class stratification system with comparative ease and that they thought of themselves as being part of that class system too. Middletown was large enough for everyone to know at least one member of each occupational group, and each group, teachers for instance, were consistently placed into a particular social class by most of the respondents. It also emerged from the Lynds' study that people tended to place their own grouping one class higher than the level at which members of other occupations put it.

More recent surveys have confirmed that most people think in terms of class structure within society and that they have well-defined senses of class consciousness. Centres[9] reports that members of his sample were able to identify with one or other of four classes – upper (three per cent claimed membership of this class), middle (forty-three per cent), working (fifty-one per cent) and lower (one per cent) – while Morris and Jeffries[10] found that people would identify with one of six classes – upper (three per cent), upper middle (twenty-two per cent), middle (fifty per cent), lower middle (five per cent), working (sixteen per cent) and lower (two per cent). While the Centres and Morris and Jeffries studies were carried out in the U.S.A., the same general pattern is apparent in Britain. In a survey by Martin,[11] ninety-six per cent of respondents were able to classify themselves, some thirty-seven per cent saying they were working class and forty-three per cent that they were middle class, nine per cent claiming to be lower class or poor.

Objective Measures of Class

In what has become a model for many measurement scales of social
class, Warner[12] presented a six-class system known as the Index of
Status Characteristics. Warner was originally involved in investigating
subjective class by means of a method he called 'evaluated
participation' which allowed respondents to evaluate the participation
of various groups in the community's affairs. The later Index of Status
Characteristics (ISC) was based on four variables differentially
weighted; these comprised: source of income (weighted 3), occupation
(weighted 4), house type (weighted 3) and dwelling area (weighted 2).
Absolute income level and education, which were also initially included
in the measure, were later dropped as they added nothing to the
predictive capability of the ISC. When people were given class positions
on the basis of both evaluated participation and the ISC, the correlation
between the two measures was found to be 0.97 while income showed
a correlation of 0.91 with the evaluated participation measure.

Warner identified specific differences in opportunity and interest
among the six American classes of the ISC and these are summarised in
Table 8.2. Taken as a whole this adds further weight to the argument
that these are definite classes rather than a continuum of socio-
economic status positions.[13] In detail, members of both the upper and
lower upper classes tend to belong to special social clubs, the men to
dining fraternities, the women to their own exclusive social cliques.
Members of these classes also tend to do social and philanthropic work
which benefits the community and emphasises the reliance of the lower
classes upon them. Their religious affiliations are typically Episcopalian
and Unitarian though some members of the top two classes may belong
to Congregational and Presbyterian churches. In all the classes whose
members can be considered 'above the Common Man' account for
thirteen per cent of the population. Those people dubbed 'the Common
Man' make up the lower middle and upper lower groups; they are in
many respects typical Americans both by number and by occupation
and life-style.

Social Class in Britain

So much of the published research concerned with social class has
emanated from the U.S.A. that specific attention to measures of class
in Britain is desirable. The measures which will be discussed here are all
based on occupational gradings of the population. Statements of class
based on occupation alone, however, have been severely criticised by
some sociologists for taking a unidimensional view of what is, almost by

Table 8.2 : Warner's Six Classes

Class	% A	% B	Description
Upper Upper	1.4	100	Old families (old to community and class); born into this class; merchants, financiers and higher professionals but have considerable inherited wealth.
Lower Upper	1.6	100	The new rich whose mobility is attributable to the new industries such as shoes and textiles and to finance. Aspire to upper upper class but wealth obtained too recently and birth to wrong class. Higher income level than any other class.
Upper Middle	10.0	88	Solid, highly respectable, 'the people who get things done'; aspire to upper classes and hope that their civic work, good deeds and morality will get them there; it seldom does. Men are typically store owners or professionals; incomes on average rather lower than for lower upper group.
Lower Middle	28.0	44	The higher level of the 'Common Man', composed of clerks, other white-collar employees; live in small houses in side streets; own their homes but little else.
Upper Lower	34.0	28	Poor but honest workers; semi- or unskilled, respectable but with limited income; the lower level of the 'Common Man'.
Lower Lower	25	26	Have a low reputation among those above them, perhaps especially among the upper lowers; thought of as lazy and shiftless but in fact are mainly just poor. Lack desire to advance, however, and this may give them their reputation, and lead to their being ranked by many below the 'Common Man' level.

Notes: %A = percentage of total population; %B = percentage of children on college preparation courses in high school.

Source: W.L. Warner *et al., Social Class in America,* Harper and Row, 1960.

definition, a multi-dimensional variable. Outside of their job roles, people in these groups might not act in a unified way or share common life-styles.[14] Further criticism of this methodology stems from the fact that occupational measures of class are generally built on the evaluation of a sample of the population of a range of jobs; they therefore reflect social status to a high degree and this may not be based entirely on economic criteria – an individual's social prestige may well remain high even though his income is decimated.

In spite of these drawbacks, it can be argued that occupational grades provide a convenient, practical and meaningful measure of social classes, at least in the context of consumer research. Monk[15] contends, for instance, with those who would substitute another variable such as income for occupation as well as with those who would use a multi-dimensional scale (embracing, say, income, education, occupation and dwelling area) and (i) the data for a substitute variable (especially income) is frequently inaccessible to the researcher, (ii) the multi-dimensional technique may involve very complex weighting systems, and (iii) such scales have no general applicability; those that are useful for consumer research stress tastes and life-styles may be inappropriate for other research fields. He concludes that the use of occupational categories is justified in marketing research because 'from a technical stand-point occupation is relatively stable and reliable at the data collection stage' and 'it is a reasonable "general purpose" classification.' Furthermore, as will be seen later, occupational groupings relate well to differences in consumer behaviour patterns regardless of income and are thereby of great marketing relevance. Indeed, despite the objections we have noted, they are extensively used in marketing research.

One of the earliest scales of occupational gradings to be put forward in Britain was proposed by Hall and Jones.[16] It is based on a list of thirty jobs which were placed in order of decreasing prestige by a sample of fourteen hundred individuals. The authors of this survey state that a considerable amount of agreement was found to exist on this ordering of occupations:

1. professional and highly administrative occupations (most members of this group had either a degree or a professional qualification);
2. managerial and executive occupations (the decision makers and policy formers);
3. (a) inspectorial, supervisory and other non-manual occupations, high grade;
   (b) inspectorial, supervisory and other non-manual occupations, lower grade;
4. skilled manual and routine white-collar occupations;
5. semi-skilled manual occupations;
6. unskilled manual occupations.

The official scheme of social grading used by the Registrar General comprises five groupings, thus:

Social Class I   Professional occupations
Social Class II   Intermediate (I and III) occupations

Social Class III   Skilled occupations
Social Class IV   Partly skilled occupations
Social Class V   Unskilled occupations

The proportion of the population belonging to each of these classes is
shown in Table 8.3.

Table 8.3 : Registrar General's Social Gradings

Registrar General's Social Grades	Proportion in the Population (%)
Social Class I (higher administration, professional and managerial)	3.0
Social Class II (other administrative, professional and managerial)	10.4
Social Class III	
(a) (shopkeepers and foremen)	7.1
(b) (clerical workers, shop assistants and skilled manual)	44.8
Social Class IV (personal service and semi-skilled manual)	15.5
Social Class V (unskilled manual)	11.3

Source: After C. Owen, *Social Stratification,* Routledge and Kegan Paul, 1968,
p. 49.

Both scales may be criticised because they tend to ignore wealth and
throw together a wide range of occupations which have little, if anything, in common. Therefore, although several physical and socio-
economic factors are associated with the jobs suggested by these
gradings, they are not used directly in consumer research. Instead a
grading scheme similar to or based on that employed for the National
Readership Survey is normally incorporated in research designs (see
Table 8.4). Monk's arguments for this scheme have already been noted
and it is interesting that a test of the scale involving (a) cross
tabulations of ratings of occupational prestige (obtained from a sample
of a thousand housewives) and (b) factor analysis of the interrelations
among the variables, corroborated these arguments in favour of using
occupations as a proxy variable for class in consumer research.[17]

Table 8.4 : National Readership Survey's Social Gradings

Grade 'A' Households — Upper Middle Class
Examples: professional and semi-professional such as physician, surgeon, architect, chartered accountant, senior civil servant, professor, newspaper editor, commercial airline pilot, chief local government officer, headmaster. Business and industry such as senior buyer, director, insurance underwriter. Police and fire such as superintendent, chief fire officer. Armed forces such as lieutenant colonel and above; naval commander and above; wing commander and above.

Grade 'B' Households — Middle Class
Examples: professional and semi-professional such as higher and senior civil servant, lecturer, qualified pharmacist, qualified accountant, newly qualified professional. Business and industry such as manager of large firms, qualified insurance clerk, general foreman, clerk of works, chief buyer. Police and fire such as chief inspector, divisional officer. Armed forces: captain, major, lieutenant, squadron leader.

Grade 'C1' Households — Lower Middle Class
Examples: professional and semi-professional such as teacher, student nurse, insurance agent, articled clerk, library assistant (not fully qualified). Business and industry such as self-employed farmer with one employee, telephonist, buyer, technician, draughtsman. Police and fire: station sergeant, leading fireman. Armed forces: sergeant, petty officer, flight sergeant.

Grade 'C2' Households — Skilled Working Class
Examples: foreman, bricklayer, carpenter, plasterer, glazier, plumber, painter, welder, minder, electrician, linotype operator, ambulance driver, maltster, prison officer, police constable, fireman, coach builder, lance corporal, leading seaman, aircraftsman.

Grade 'D' Households — Unskilled Working Class
Examples: labourer, mate of occupations listed in C2 grade, fisherman, gardener, bottler, opener, cleaner, traffic warden, bus conductor, porter.

Grade 'E' Households — Those at Lowest Level of Subsistence
Examples: casual labourer, part-time worker, old age pensioner.

(All occupations refer to work of the household head.)

Source: Derived from D. Monk, *Social Grading on the National Readership Survey*, JICNARS, 1973.

Class and the Customer

Social class is directly related to a large proportion of consumer decision making including product and brand usage patterns, the frequency of shopping trips, interpersonal consumer relationships and innovative behaviour. Martineau[18] pointed out almost twenty years ago that there is a discernible social class system at work in urban markets, that there are extensive psychological variations from class to class and that consumption patterns may reflect attempts at defining

class membership through the use of symbols of prestige. He also
asserted that class is more forceful a factor in consumer behaviour than
income alone. His findings on class-related different motivational
characteristics which were commented on in Chapter 3 are presented
fully in Table 8.5. Other dimensions of the social class—consumer
choice relationship are dealt with below.

Table 8.5 : Social Class and Motivation

Orientation	Middle Class	Lower Class
Cognitive	More abstract in his thinking, stresses rationality and has a well-structured idea of the universe.	Much more concrete in his thinking, essentially non-rational, vague structuring of the world.
Temporal	Outlook embraces a long time-span, pointed to the future.	Lives, thinks, behaves within the limitation of a short-time period, pointed to past and present.
Place	Greater urban identification.	Greater rural identification.
Self-perception	Understands himself as connected with national happenings.	Life revolves around his family.
General Outlook	Extended horizons, enhanced sense of making choices, willing to take risks.	Limited sense of choice making, limited horizons concerned with security and stability.

Source: Derived from P. Martineau, 'Social classes and spending behaviour',
Journal of Marketing, 23, 1958.

Product Usage and Brand Choice

Differences between the social classes can be isolated for a wide range
of product usage patterns. Table 8.6 shows the relationships between
class and dentifrice purchases. A clear pattern of product usage rates
can be seen for the classes with respect to all users and heavy users and
this type of information can provide the basis for market segmentation.
Differential patterns of brand preference are also discernible for many
other products. In the case of biscuit consumption in the U.K., for
instance, there are clear variations in the choice of types and brands of
biscuit.[19] Higher class consumers show a slight preference for plain
biscuits, lower class buyers for cream biscuits, but the patterns for
assorted and chocolate-coated varieties are similar from one class to
another. Weston biscuits have a distinctly upper class appeal and Jacobs
also appeal more to higher class than lower class individuals.

Table 8.6 : Social Class and Product Usage Patterns — Dentifrice

Social Class	All Buyers (%)	Heavy Buyers (%)
AB	12	17
C1	24	15
C2	41	49
DE	22	19

Source: AGB Research Ltd, 'Audit' 2, 2, 1972.

Cooperative Wholesale Society, Marks and Spencer (*St. Michael*) and loose unbranded biscuits have a greater working class appeal. Some other brands — Peak Frean and McVities — seem to draw customers from all classes. Information such as this provides the starting point for market segmentation analysis and the identification of consumer tastes and class appeal is not only important for the product itself but also for promotion and advertising.

Pre-purchase Information Sources

Several studies of various products have shown that there are considerable class variations in sources of pre-purchase information. In one example, Rich and Jain[20] reported their analysis of data from over one thousand personal interviews 'with a probability sample representing all women twenty years of age or older residing in the Cleveland standard metropolitan statistical area'. The measure of social class employed was a variation of Warner's Index of Status Character- istics, education and income level being substituted for house type and source of income. The authors found that a substantial proportion of all classes sought information from newspapers and magazines with respect to fashion purchases, and they conclude that 'Women in various social classes seemed to find newspaper ads helpful to about the same degree'.

A study among housewives in Newcastle upon Tyne, which was partly a replication of Rich and Jain's work, also employed a modified ISC measure of social class, dwelling area being the main preliminary variable used to establish two classes, middle and lower.[21] The remaining criteria were satisfied by the inclusion of questions relating to the household's source of income and the occupation of the head of household on the interview schedule. Although it is not a variable normally included in the ISC nowadays, the education of the household head was also requested, firstly as a check on the other data (education is a useful correlate of class) and secondly to ensure greater comparability with the results obtained by Rich and Jain.

With respect to pre-purchase sources of information relating to the purchase of domestic appliances, the Newcastle data show that only seven per cent of the lower class respondents and twelve per cent of the middle class respondents used newspaper and magazine advertisements. Not only are these rather low proportions absolutely compared with those reported by Rich and Jain, but they are also significantly different. The discrepancy between the British and American data may stem, in part, from differences between the product groups used in each study (see Table 8.7). At the same time it is well known that American periodicals carry more advertising than their British counterparts.

Table 8.7 : Newspapers as Pre-purchase Information Sources

Class (%)	Fashion Items	Domestic Appliances	Class (%)
Upper upper	91		
Lower upper	67		
Upper middle	68	12	Middle
Lower middle	60		
Upper lower	57	7	Lower
Lower lower	39		

Sources: Derived from S.U. Rich and S.C. Jain, 'Social class and life cycle as predictors of shopping behaviour', *Journal of Marketing Research*, 5, 1968; G.R. Foxall, 'Social factors in consumer choice', *Journal of Consumer Research*, 2, 1, 1975.

Other significant differences were apparent from the Newcastle survey; middle class respondents were more likely to obtain information from brochures and leaflets and from their friends and neighbours than were the lower class buyers. The latter relied heavily on in-store sources of information (mainly from salesmen and women). Finally, while twelve per cent of the middle class sample reported that they had consulted *Which?*, none of the lower class respondents claimed to have done so.

Shopping Frequency

Shopping frequency has been found to vary significantly with social class; this conclusion was borne out by both of the studies cited above and is confirmed in a number of geographical surveys. Rich and Jain's evidence showed that thirty-eight per cent of women in the upper class and thirty-four per cent in the middle class shopped fifty-two or more times per year, that is, once or more a week on average, compared with twenty-four per cent in the lower class.[22] The Newcastle data refer this time to shopping trips for grocery products, and show that middle class respondents were more likely to shop twice weekly (sixty-two per cent of them did so compared with thirty-nine per cent of lower class people) while lower class respondents were more likely to shop once weekly (sixty per cent compared with thirty-seven). This last result is contrary to some expectations about middle class and working class shopping frequencies (which show that the lower the social class, the higher the frequency of grocery shopping) and may be explicable in terms of the availability of retail outlets in the two areas, the patterns of female working in the town and the availability of transportation.[23]

Interpersonal Communication and Influence

Being accompanied by others on shopping trips and discussing purchases with one's family are not in themselves proof of reference group influence but they strongly suggest its presence. Cleveland women's shopping behaviour does not appear to have been significantly influenced by others though there was a slight tendency for their husbands to be more influential if they were upper or middle class than if they were lower class.[24] In contrast, Newcastle husbands were found to exert a considerable class-related influence, as is shown in Tables 8.8 and 8.9. The belief that the principal differences between the British and American analyses derives from the different product categories used in each survey is corroborated by the fact that among Newcastle families no significant differences were apparent between the proportion of housewives from each class who discussed the purchase of domestic appliances with their husbands (seventy-eight per cent of middle class housewives reported that they did this compared with seventy-three per cent of lower class respondents); but a significant difference was apparent in the case of groceries (Table 8.9).

The tables concentrate on the interaction of housewives with their husbands because significant relationships were found here but they were absent in the cases of children, mothers and friends. Nevertheless, a significant difference was found to exist with respect to people other than these, presumably sisters and other relatives and neighbours who were not classed as friends (Table 8.10). In both cases — shopping accompaniment and discussions — lower class women interacted far more with these 'others' than did middle class housewives.[25] This can be explained by reference to Bott's work on the family[26] which suggests that working class communities are far more close-knit than middle class communities, being characterised by much greater interpersonal contact between friends, neighbours and relatives. (Other

Table 8.8 : Proportion of Housewives who Shop with Husbands (%)

	Groceries	*Domestic Appliances*
Middle Class	9 (n=298)	60 (n=278)
Lower Class	19 (n=286)	49 (n=236)

Table 8.9 : Proportion of Housewives who Discuss Grocery Purchases with Husband (%)

Middle Class	17 (n=298)
Lower Class	27 (n=286)

Table 8.10 : Effect of 'Other' Relatives and Acquaintances

		% Shopping with 'Others'	*% Discussing Grocery Purchases with 'Others'*
	Groceries	*Domestic Appliances*	
Middle Class	1	4	9
Lower Class	13	9	25

Source: G.R. Foxall, 'Social factors in consumer choice', *Journal of Consumer Research,* 2, 1, 1975.

family differences between classes, particularly with respect to the family life cycle, were discussed in Chapter 7).

There were also significant differences between classes concerning shopping alone and discussing purchases with no one. Some forty-five per cent of lower class women shopped alone for groceries compared with sixty-two per cent of middle class respondents; no significant differences appeared in the case of domestic appliances, but while twenty-nine per cent of lower class housewives discussed their grocery purchases with no one, some fifty-three per cent of middle class respondents came into this category.

Social Classes and Innovation

There is some evidence that social classes differ from each other in another important respect which is relevant to consumer behaviour – the adoption of innovations. Graham[27] conducted a survey among families in Connecticut to determine their willingness to adopt five innovations – television, canasta, supermarkets, and two items referring to medical insurance plans. Twenty-five members of each of six social classes were interviewed and, as the data in Table 8.11 indicate, conservatism in the adoption of particular innovations varies

Table 8.11 : Social Class and the Adoption of Innovations

Class		Adopters in each class * (%)		
		Television	Canasta	Supermarkets
Upper	I	24	72	52
	II	44	72	80
Middle	III	48	44	56
	IV	52	20	80
Lower	V	84	32	52
	VI	72	12	48

* Criteria of adoption : television — ownership of a set
canasta — having played more than once
supermarkets — obtaining over half of one's food there

Source: Derived from S. Graham, 'Class and conservatism in the adoption of innovations', *Human Relations*, 9, 1956.

considerably from one class to another. As far as television was concerned, the upper classes were most conservative about its adoption; canasta was least attractive to those in the lower class; and supermarkets had the greatest appeal to middle class individuals, members of other classes showing conservatism as far as this innovation was concerned. No significant differences in adoption ratio were discovered in the case of health insurance.

Changes in Classes and Consumer Behaviour

An issue which has provoked much discussion among sociologists and the implications of which impinge on consumer research is that of the alleged 'embourgeoisement' of the affluent working classes. The sustained levels of affluence achieved in countries such as Great Britain and the U.S.A. in the decades immediately following the Second World War led some social commentators to propose the idea that formerly working class individuals were acquiring material goods usually associated with middle class life-styles, they were also acquiring middle class values and were being accepted into middle class residential communities. As a result, it was argued, the traditional working class was disappearing and the majority of employed people were said to be middle class. In Britain, the continued presence of a Conservative Government was taken as evidence that a shift in working class values and allegiances had taken place.

Goldthorpe *et al.* [28] subjected this to rigorous empirical testing and concluded that it had little to commend it. The evidence from which they rejected the embourgeoisement thesis is threefold. First, although the incomes of many manual workers have undoubtedly improved in terms of take-home pay, the manual worker has not advanced much in terms of the total economic rewards he receives. Payments throughout the overall working lives are much greater for most white-collar workers who also have better pension rights, job security and other financial advantages. Secondly, working class people do not seem to be losing their traditional values and beliefs; they have not switched en masse to voting Conservative and still support trade unionism. Thirdly, working class social relationships show little sign of fundamental change since family contacts seem to be unaltered despite increased social and geographical mobility and the traditional middle classes do not appear to want to admit manual workers into their social clubs or social lives.[29]

Sociologically, then, the embourgeoisement thesis cannot be substantiated but the behaviour it attempts to explain is still of significance to marketing for it points to the existence of a growing group of affluent workers whose material life-style is essentially and increasingly middle class. It is undoubtedly true, as Goldthorpe *et al.* continually stress, that class membership is determined by relationships rather than acquisitions, but their work and that of other social scientists identifies a group of 'socially-marginal' consumers who are increasingly home-centred and 'privatised'. This group may be too large and heterogeneous to compose a single market segment but its existence has implications for marketing generally and for each element of the marketing mix particularly. Advertising and promotional efforts may be directed specifically at this group's desires for a home-centred life and, within this group, there is undoubtedly a market segment composed of those who do aspire to middle class membership and whose values and behaviour are less and less identifiable as working class and more and more 'bourgeois'. This could be an important segment of most consumer goods markets and will continue to be a growing one in terms of both numbers and disposable income.

Applications

Market Segmentation

The most obvious application of social class—consumer behaviour relationships to marketing management has been mentioned several times already in this chapter. The ideas which underpin segmentation analysis have undergone some changes in recent years but it is not long since there was some debate in the marketing literature about the relative advantages of using socio-demographic criteria or psychographic variables as the bases for marketing strategies.[30] While a firm is usually under pressure not to miss out on the possibilities offered in the market-place for a segmental approach, there is always a danger of false segmentation which arises from identified segments being too small to support profitable production and marketing. This is especially likely in the case of an over-enthusiastic psychographic approach to segmentation. The chapters on personality showed that psychological variables, despite superficial relevance to marketing behaviour, are often not strongly related to specific consumer choices.

The relevance of social class to marketing has been demonstrated in this chapter and the overall opinion among marketing writers is that the use of socio-demographic criteria provides a safer approach to segmentation analysis and practice. This is not to rule out psychographic criteria — for there are sometimes special opportunities to be exploited — but one needs to be cautious about their use. The increasingly important 'life-style' segmentation relies heavily on the consumer's social situation.

Consumer Loyalty

Building up consumer loyalty which leads to repeat sales is a fundamental objective of all companies. Yet attempts at identifying the behavioural correlates of brand loyalty and store loyalty have produced inauspicious results. A study carried out by Ennis and Paul[31] which involved sixteen psychological variables led to the conclusion that none of these was significantly related to loyalty. Several examinations of this area have, however, discovered an inverse relationship between social class and consumer loyalty. Ennis and Paul, for instance, note that consumers of lower educational or occupational status tend to be more loyal than those from higher social groups. Carman[32] conducted a survey which led him to conclude that 'the loyal consumer is the busy woman who typically is working to help support a family' — another indication that loyalty is associated with a lower class position: buying has become habitual presumably for reasons of convenience. Again, Schapker has demonstrated that members of lower social classes are more bound to habitual buying behaviour than are their middle class counterparts.[33]

Store Patronage

This is a closely related phenomenon to product or brand loyalty and it has been said that social class is the 'most important variable affecting store patronisation'.[34] This is one of the fields where marketing geographers have contributed enormously to our understanding of consumer decision making and preferences and it has been pointed out that customers' preferences are not simply a reflection of income or prices; consumers are willing to pay more if the atmosphere of the store suits their expectations, and these are shaped to a large extent by class considerations.[35]

Diffusion of New Products

Since the pioneering work of Rogers, which was referred to in Chapter 6, considerable work has been conducted which examines the social position of innovators. It was pointed out earlier that innovative doctors have certain socio-psychological characteristics and Graham's research has demonstrated that the acceptance of innovative products is a class-related phenomenon.[36]

Summary

Social class refers to economic divisions in society into which individuals can be categorised by means of such proxy variables for class as occupation, income or source of income, education and residential location. Status is the honour or prestige which society in general accords to the occupant of a given social position. Both class and status carry the idea of a hierarchy of positions.

Social class can be measured both subjectively and objectively. Most people have a fairly clear-cut idea of a system of social stratification and of their own place and others' places within it. Lloyd Warner's Index of Status Characteristics provides a useful objective measurement and has formed the basis of many social investigations and consumer research projects. In Britain, the Registrar General's system of social grading and the Hall–Jones scale have been widely employed; both depend on occupation to determine social class and this is criticised by many writers. Nevertheless the arguments in favour of occupational grading for consumer research are strong ones and the type of scale used by the National Readership Survey (which involves six classes: A, B, C1, C2, D and E) is extensively used in marketing investigations.

Social class is associated with several facets of consumer behaviour including product usage, brand preference, the choice of information sources, shopping frequency and innovative behaviour. These provide possibilities for market segmentation policies to be planned and implemented but it must be remembered that not all of these class-related effects apply to all product groups and that segmentation, to be really successful, must be based on more than one variable — preferably several interrelated social/demographic and psychographic variables.

Notes

1. J.F. Engel *et al.*, *Consumer Behaviour*, Holt, Rinehart and Winston, 1973, Chapter 5.
2. S. Cotgrove, *The Science of Society*, Unwin, 1972, p. 218.
3. P.F. Berger, *Invitation to Sociology: A Humanistic Perspective*, Penguin Books, 1965, p. 95.
4. J. Rex and R. Moore, *Race Community and Conflict*, Oxford University Press, 1967, p. 36.
5. Berger, *Invitation to Sociology*.
6. H. Gerth and C.W. Mills, *From Max Weber: Essays in Sociology*, Routledge and Kegan Paul, 1948, p. 193.
7. R. Brown, *Social Psychology*, Free Press, 1965, p. 103.
8. R.S. Lynd and H.M. Lynd, *Middletown*, Harcourt Brace and World, 1929.
9. R. Centres, 'The American class structure: a psychological analysis', in C.E. Swanson *et al.* (eds), *Readings in Social Psychology*, Holt, Rinehart and Winston, 1952.
10. R.T. Morris and V. Jeffries, 'Class conflict: forget it!' *Sociology and Social Research*, 54, 1970.
11. See D.V. Glass (ed.), *Social Mobility in Britain*, Routledge and Kegan Paul, 1954.
12. W.L. Warner, *Social Class in America*, Harper and Row, 1960.
13. Brown, *Social Psychology*, Chapter 3.
14. J. Rex, 'The changing national class structure', in E. Butterworth and D. Weir (eds), *The Sociology of Modern Britain*, Fontana, 1970.
15. D. Monk, *Social Grading on the National Readership Survey*, JICNARS, 1973.
16. J. Hall and D.C. Jones, 'The social grading of occupations', *British Journal of Sociology*, 1, 1950.
17. Monk, *Social Grading on the N.R.S.*
18. P. Martineau, 'Social classes and spending behaviour', *Journal of Marketing*, 23, 1958.
19. J.R.G. Jenkins, *Marketing and Customer Behaviour*, Pergamon, 1972, p. 61.
20. S.U. Rich and S.C. Jain, 'Social class and life cycle as predictors of shopping behaviour', *Journal of Marketing Research*, 5, 1968.
21. G.R. Foxall, 'Social factors in consumer choice: replication and extension', *Journal of Consumer Research*, 2, 1, 1975.
22. Rich and Jain, 'Social class and life cycle', p. 44.
23. Foxall, 'Social factors in consumer choice', p. 63.
24. Rich and Jain, 'Social class and life cycle', pp. 43–4.
25. Foxall, 'Social factors in consumer choice', p. 64.
26. E. Bott, *Family and Social Network*, Tavistock, 1960.
27. S. Graham, 'Class conservatism in the adoption of innovations', *Human Relations*, 9, 1956.
28. J.H. Goldthorpe *et al.*, *The Affluent Worker in the Class Structure*, Cambridge University Press, 1969.
29. M. Young and P. Willmott, *Family and Class in a London Suburb*, Routledge and Kegan Paul, 1960.

30.   D. Yankelovich, 'New criteria for market segmentation', *Harvard Business Review*, 42, 1964; W. Reynolds, 'More sense about segmentation', *Harvard Business Review*, 43, 1965.

31.   B.M. Ennis and G.W. Paul, 'Store loyalty as a basis for market segmentation', *Journal of Retailing*, Fall 1970.

32.   J.M. Carman, 'Correlates of brand loyalty', *Journal of Marketing Research*, 7, 1970.

33.   B.L. Shapker, 'Behaviour patterns of supermarket shoppers', *Journal of Marketing*, 30, 1966.

34.   R.L. Davies, *Patterns and Profiles of Consumer Behaviour*, Newcastle University Department of Geography, 1973, p. 11.

35.   R.L. Davies, *Marketing Geography*, Retailing and Planning Associates, 1976.

36.   D.F. Midgley, *Innovation and New Product Development*, Croom Helm, 1977.

9 CULTURES AND SUBCULTURES

So far we have understood consumer behaviour to be a function of the individual and his social system but another factor which exerts a notable influence on the consumer is *culture*. Because culture has a general effect on behaviour, its components are often taken for granted and even to the behavioural scientist culture sometimes seems to be a rather vague sort of influence. Its ramifications are, however, as real as those of the institutions through which it is mediated, the family, the social stratification system, education, and so on. Indeed, not a few firms have had disastrous results through underestimating the power of peculiarities in consumption patterns within different cultures. Others have enjoyed great success through using such peculiarities to advance the position of their products in foreign cultures and among domestic subcultures. This chapter discusses the meaning of culture and its relevance to modern marketing practice.

The Meaning of Culture

Definitions of culture should not be difficult to find; behavioural scientists have produced literally dozens of them. Some examples of definitions are:

..... that complex whole which includes knowledge, belief, art morals, law, custom and other capabilities acquired by man as a member of society. (Tylor[1])

..... abstract patterns of and for living and dying. Such abstract patterns are cultural to the extent that they are learned directly or indirectly in social interaction and to the extent that they are part of the common orientation of two or more people. (Johnson[2])

..... the configuration of learned behaviour and results of behaviour whose component elements are shared and transmitted by the members of a particular society (Linton[3])

In order to understand more fully the implications of culture for marketing purposes it is worth while analysing the assumptions which underpin its definition and the elements which compose it. While Murdock[4] claimed that there are seven assumptions to be found in the

159

definition of culture (that it is learned, inculcated, social, ideational, gratifying, adaptive and integrative) Moore and Lewis have narrowed these down to two: 'for anything to be an item of culture', they say, 'it must be, first, a learned response, and, second, it must be a response learned by at least one individual from at least one other individual'.[5] Table 9.1 presents their arguments for disposing with Murdock's other assumptions.

Table 9.1 : Assumptions of Culture

Assumed Characteristics	*Evaluation*
Culture is learned: it does not result from instinct or physical inheritance but from social interaction and socialisation	True; but not all learned responses stem from culture.
Culture is inculcated: while all animals learn, only man seems to be capable of transmitting his habits to his young.	The term culture need not be confined to things passed on from parents to children: 'whether a response learned from others is a permanent part of the response repertoire, whether it was learned in a single trial or many trials, whether it was 'taught' or 'just picked up somehow', it is an 'item of culture',
Culture is social: 'that is, shared by human beings living in organised aggregates or societies and kept relatively uniform by social pressures'.	Social pressure may also fail to maintain uniformity of culture; 'uniformity is not a necessary condition'. Further, culture does not confine itself to matters that all members of a society share.
Culture is ideational: it includes language and symbolic behaviour.	The first assumption includes this one.
Culture is gratifying: it satisfies physical needs and derived needs.	A learned response does not continue to be gratifying; therefore, not all culture is gratifying.
Culture is adaptive: it is capable of changing in a way analogous to organic evolution.	Not all cultures are evolutionary; they do not all develop; some die; most have an ability to survive but this is not a necessary condition of culture.
Culture is integrative: there is a tendency for culture to be integrative and for its elements to form a consistent whole.	Since this is only something that a culture tends to do, it cannot be an all-time necessary condition. Cultures differ in the extent of their integratedness and some are marked by conflict.

Sources: Derived from G.P. Murdock, 'Uniformities in culture', *American Sociological Review*, 5, 1940; O.K. Moore and D.J. Lewis, 'Learning theory and culture', *Psychological Review*, 59, 1952.

Johnson[6] has suggested a classification of the essential elements of
culture with which most social scientists would agree. It comprises:

1. *Cognitive elements* which are knowledge of the physical and social
worlds, science, technology, practical knowledge transmitted from one
generation to the next, ideas about social organisation and the way in
which society works.

2. *Beliefs* which, unlike cognitive elements of culture, are not capable
of empirical validation or refutation, *e.g.* religious beliefs and systems
of magic; beliefs are interwoven with cognitive elements of culture and
scientific analysis may be necessary to separate the two.

3. *Values and norms*, values being consensus views about the kind of
life individuals should follow, the goals they should pursue; clearly
these ideas differ markedly from society to society — competition with
one's fellow man is highly regarded in some cultures and incurs severe
sanctions in others. Norms are defined in two ways: first, they refer to
patterns of ideal behaviour which a society rewards (reinforces, in the
terminology of learning theory); secondly, a norm is a description of
the behaviour of the majority of a social system's members.

4. *Signs* which include signals and symbols. Signals indicate the
existence or presence of a thing, occurrence or condition,[7] *e.g.* a bell
may signal that dinner is ready or that a boxing match is about to
begin; street signs, sounds, pictures may all serve as signals. Symbols are
usually verbal in nature and refer to concepts, and languages are
systems of symbols which facilitate communication but which differ
considerably from society to society.

5. *Non-normative behaviour* denotes ways of acting which involve the
individual's personal reaction and response to the culture in which he
lives; individual predispositions and personality traits determine non-
normative behaviour which is not openly punished by society unless it
becomes so extreme that it threatens to transgress some norm, more
or folkway — even eccentric behaviour is allowed by most people to
continue only when it falls within fairly closely defined limits.

Cultural Universals

Writers on culture normally tend to stress the differences which exist
between cultures but there is a large number of areas in which cultural

norms seem to be remarkably similar in all known societies. These cultural universals include age grading, athletics, bodily adornment, cleanliness, courtship, cosmology, dream interpretation, education, ethics, etiquette, faith healing, funeral rites, incest taboos, marriage, property rights, religious ritual, status differentiation, surgery, tool making, weather control, and so forth.[8]

Although these general characteristics are to be found in all societies, it is evident that their form differs from one to another — marriage, for example, has many different forms as does language. But despite the different forms taken by cultural factors, so many are common to all societies that the manager's job is made slightly easier because demand for many consumer products spreads far beyond any particular society and arises from the same motivational forces. The usual approach to culture and marketing stresses the converse of this, that it is the cultural differences between markets that are of most importance. Of course, these differentials can be very important and later in this chapter they will be examined, but it is worth remembering that a firm's market may extend far beyond the limits of its present field of operations and that many demand factors in other cultures are likely to be surprisingly similar.

Subcultures

Large groups within society may be referred to as subcultures if they are sub-societies which embrace both sexes, all age groups and institutions found in the total society.[9] In practice, the term subculture is used less strictly than this and refers to any group which has discernible characteristics that make it worth considering separately from the overall society in which it exists. Subcultures may thus be determined on the basis of religion, area or region of residence, social class or ethnic grouping, and we speak of the teenager subculture, the Negro subculture, and so on.

Subcultures are important for marketing since consumer behaviour often varies from one to another and some subcultures are based almost entirely on cultural artifacts which are obtained in the marketing system — Hell's Angels, for example, define membership, at least in part, by the ownership of certain accoutrements — motor cycle, helmet, leather jacket, etc. Additionally, there are motor cycle enthusiast clubs which, while they may not constitute subcultures in the accepted sense, are based entirely on ownership of consumer durables. Camera clubs and many other informal associations are also based on this same characteristic.[10]

Culture and Consumer Behaviour

Several aspects of culture impinge on consumer behaviour and are of significance for the marketing manager. The following section summarises the major findings which behavioural scientists have reported about cultural influences on behaviour and assesses their relevance to marketing management.

Culture and Perception

What individuals perceive of their world is not a result of physical factors alone or even of their motives and attitudes. It depends also on 'cultural frames of reference' and the interpretation of whatever items are perceived varies according to the cultural framework into which it is fitted by the perceiver. For example, the cultural meanings which members of European, Asian and North American societies might attach to their first observation of a soccer match in Britain would vary enormously. Krech and Crutchfield[11] have provided the example of a Mexican bullfight of which the Mexican native perceives the performer's skill and bravery while an American tourist might notice only the pain of the animal, the smell and the flies. Cultural context is important, therefore, because it supplies the meanings which become attached to objects, events and states, and these meanings, as was shown in Chapter 2, determine the interpretation of whatever is perceived.

Closely related to the question of how perception is affected by culture is the influence of ethnocentrism. This derives from the tendency shown by nearly all peoples of assuming that their own way of looking at the world is somehow 'right' or 'proper' or the only way of perceiving the universe. The ideas of foreigners are thought to be suspect or simply wrong by those who show high levels of ethnocentrism because their own culture is taken so much for granted. Ethnocentrism is especially virulent with respect to food preferences, table manners, toilet habits, health practices and patterns of sexual behaviour, while religious training exerts a pervasively influential role in establishing culturally appropriate ways of perceiving, thinking and behaving.[12]

Most consumers faced with products which originate in other cultures are simply not willing to go through the process of wondering whether their own cultural expectations are necessarily universally 'right', finding out about the meanings attached to the product in another culture and making an effort to comprehend the product in a new light. By far the easier thing to do is to select products which are familiar and the meanings of which are readily apparent and to reject those that are strange and the meanings of which are ambiguous. The vast majority of consumers react in this manner and there have been some spectacular cases of products failing in overseas cultures (despite being extremely successful in their domestic markets) simply because their marketing managers failed to understand the cultural imperatives involved in their overseas operations.

A clear example is an American attempt at promoting margarine in Spain as a substitute for butter which failed because the usage rate for butter in Spain is low and cooking oil is a cheap alternative to both butter and margarine.[13] Even where cultures are superficially similar, however, the meanings attached to the same product can vary immensely from one society to another. An attempt at introducing to Britain an American brand of apple pie which was very popular in the United States failed simply because British consumers would not accept it.[14]

Consumer acceptance is not the only reason for product failures where different cultures are concerned; managements may misjudge other aspects of the newly penetrated society such as the availability of finance. But the question of whether consumers will go out and buy a 'foreign' item depends often on how well the firm marketing it has done its homework and has identified consumer tastes and explained the meaning of its products unambiguously to those who are expected to buy them. Finding a new meaning for such products may be the only way to obtain sales and this means fully understanding the new culture and the ways of its people. Mistakes often result from assuming that there are great similarities between cultures where these are strictly limited. Wine consumption in France (*per capita*) is, for instance, some three-and-a-half times that in Belgium while *per capita* beer consumption in France is less than a sixth that in Belgium despite the shared language and other cultural factors which are common to inhabitants of both countries.[15] Kassarjian and Robertson[16] have pointed out several mistaken beliefs about foreign cultures which are difficult to dispel: chop suey is essentially a Chinese dish; pizzas are Italian in origin but have undergone a partial metamorphosis in America; the type of soap referred to by Americans as 'French' is, in fact, used by just one fifth of French women.

Signals and Symbols: Anthropology in Marketing?

Signs, which include signals and symbols, were identified above as essential parts of any culture. Anthropologists, whose special study is of culture, are well aware of the meanings attached to the various signs in differing societies and it has even been suggested that anthropology has a profound contribution to make to marketing management.[17] Anthropologists, it is suggested, could inform managers about the meanings attached to signals and symbols, of the significance of 'rites de passage' and of the part played by taboos in the lives of members of a particular culture. As examples of this: an anthropologist has helped a manufacturer of heating systems by pointing out the symbolism of fire in the folk lore of the intended consumers; another saved a shirt manufacturer who was about to advertise men's shirts in women's magazines because women bought over half of his output by pointing out that studies of husband—wife interaction showed that men were beginning to resent this; and a third anthropologist helped a shoe manufacturer to see that, for the child of four or six, being able to tie up his own shoes is a landmark in personal development, 'and to assist the manufacturer in developing methods for using the relationship between shoes and "rites de passage" '.

Without denying the practicalities of such bits of knowledge — some of the specific taboos which Winick mentions in his article are summarised in Table 9.2 — it seems evident that marketing does not need anthropology as such, though some of its insights are useful. Many of the facts which it is claimed are strictly anthropological should be brought out by fairly rigorous marketing research and by knowledge of local behaviour and customs gained from nationals.

Table 9.2 : Some Cultural Taboos of Marketing Significance

Society	Symbol	Meaning of Association
Iran	Blue	Funereal colour, mourning
Egypt, Syria	Green	Nationalist colour
Gold Coast	Pairs of items	Disapproved
Japan	White	Colour of mourning
Nicaragua	Brown, grey	Disapproved
Latin America	Purple	Death
Thailand	Feet	Regarded as despicable

Source: Derived from C. Winick, 'Anthropology's contributions to marketing', *Journal of Marketing*, 25, 1961.

In one of the examples just cited, knowledge of the market research literature would have prevented the shirt manufacturer from making a mistake. So, while not denying that anthropologists may from time to time have knowledge which would otherwise be inaccessible to the manager, there seems no more case for recommending that marketing should incorporate the scientific study of anthropology into its body of knowledge than for claiming that gardeners require expert knowledge of geology. The knowledge gained from anthropologists or knowledgeable marketing researchers which refers to the symbolic meaning of colours and artifacts in a different culture from that which the marketer is familiar can, of course, be of great practical value – packaging and product colours can be decided upon sensibly when such knowledge is available but this is by no means the same thing as introducing formal courses in anthropology into the marketing syllabus.

Cross-cultural Comparisons

There have been few comparisons of the effects of two or more cultures on consumer decision making reported in the marketing literature, indicating that there is a great deal of empirical work still remaining to be done in this area. Nevertheless, a survey by Hempel[18] of family decision-making processes in Hartford, Connecticut and in Preston, Lancaster provides valuable information on how culture permeates the institutions of a society and impinges on consumer behaviour. Hempel's study is similar to that of Davis and Rigaux which was discussed in Chapter 7 in that it investigates four types of family role structure (husband-dominated, wife-dominated, syncratic and autonomic) during three stages of the decision making process (the initiation of a product idea, information-seeking and purchase decision phases). The survey was concerned, however, with the purchase of a house and each of the responding families had recently taken this step.

During the initiating phase, it appears to be the husband, in both societies, who plays the major role and this confirms previous evidence relating to other products. But Hempel found a considerably greater tendency for the husband to be the idea initiator in England than in America and the differences between these cultures was statistically significant. The role of information seeker was jointly performed in both samples for a majority of families and there is a considerable degree of consistency in the proportion of cases for which jointly held roles were apparent in both cultures (fifty-six per cent of cases in America compared with fifty-four in Britain). Making the final decision to buy also tended to be jointly performed in both cultures but there were some variations within this general pattern from decision area to decision area. For example, while neighbourhood and house-style decisions were reported as jointly taken in three-quarters of cases, fewer than half the families claimed that the choice of a source of mortgage was joint. Both men and women respondents reported more joint overall decision making in England than in America.

This survey is useful in showing that cross-cultural research can be fitted into existing typologies of consumer behaviour and in emphasising the similarities and differences that exist from one culture to another. But there are many product areas where our knowledge of the effects of culture are very sketchy and replication of this type of research is imperative if a wider picture of cultural influences on the consumer is to be built up.

More will be said later of the effects of poverty on consumer choices but this aspect of behaviour is worth mentioning here as another example of cross-cultural research. From work by Kaynak,[19] there appears to be some similarity between low-income consumers in Istanbul and the so-called 'ghetto' consumers of the United States. For instance, despite the fact that it might be more economical to shop further afield, both groups of poor consumers show a marked preference for the food outlets in the immediate vicinity of their homes. Both groups also have favourable attitudes towards business firms and practices and tend to confine their buying behaviour to local stores in order to reinforce their cultural expectations of the buying situation. That is, they shop where they are accepted and treated fairly.

Some differences between these groups were apparent, however — for example, the low-income families of Istanbul spend a higher proportion of their income on food than is the case among poor Americans — but both groups are said to share a need for consumer education. Kaynak recommends that the media be used more effectively to inform poor consumers of low-price retail outlets but this assumes that the consumer behaviour of such consumers shows great price-sensitivity and ignores the cultural barriers that may be faced if consumers are encouraged to switch to new outlets.

Subcultures and Consumer Preferences

Knowledge of subcultures within a company's domestic or overseas markets can clearly provide sound bases for differential marketing policies and strategies. However, this requires penetrating marketing research which identifies the behavioural criteria on which a segmental approach can be based and a non-superficial picture of the extent of the subculture's influences on consumption preferences and the exact nature of buyer wants within the market segment. A common mistake is to assume that a so-called subculture is more homogeneous than it really is and to miss the obvious segments which exist within a sub-society. It is usual, for example, to think that the Negro subculture in the United States consists of the entire eleven per cent of that population who are Negroes. In fact, there may well be no such thing as 'the Negro subculture' as a distinct entity and, certainly as far as marketing is concerned, there is no single Negro market. Northern educated blacks have a very different life-style and pattern of consumer wants from those of southern, rural Negroes.[20] While the executives of North American firms have been aware of this for some time, there is evidence that European and other marketers are only now beginning to exploit the possibilities afforded by several ethnic cultures in the United States.

Ethnic Subcultures

The marketing implications of subcultures can best be illustrated through reference to ethnic groups because this is the area in which most research has been carried out and because ethnic subcultures are frequently much more important to the marketing manager than those based on religion, class or region (though these factors are also often present in the cases of ethnic subgroups).

An accurate impression of the complexities involved in marketing to subcultures emerges from Alexander's account[21] of the reactions of members of Italian, Jewish, Negro and Puerto Rican subgroups in Greater New York to six new products: frozen dinners, frozen red meat, frozen fruit pie, instant coffee, cake mixes and dehydrated soups. Despite pressures towards conformity, each of these groups (which collectively account for fifty-five per cent of the population of Greater New York) has managed to maintain its cultural independence and this is reflected in differential eating habits and rates of acceptance of new food products. Italian housewives show a notable disinclination to adopt processed, frozen or packaged grocery items and prefer freshness. The vast majority of Jewish housewives also prefer fresh foods to tinned or frozen varieties and have strong traditional ties with their own speciality foods. Negroes have traditional preferences for meat as a breakfast food, for starchy foods and for non-raw foods but, especially among the younger generation, accept convenience foods as a mark of status. Finally, Puerto Ricans, despite their strong traditional ties to certain foods, seem to be more flexible in their eating habits for they had tried all of the convenience items involved in this test and frequently use them as a complement to their established diets.

Table 9.3 : Responses of New York Subcultures to Convenience Foods

	Jewish	*Puerto Rican*	*Negro*	*Italian*
Frozen Dinners	Dislike taste and price; no large-scale acceptance; last in order of preference	Lead all groups in consumption rates because working housewives desire convenience	Resist on traditional grounds; wide usage but small quantities	Prefer fresh meat and vegetables; lowest consumption rates of all groups
Frozen Red Meat	Dietary laws militate against use. especially in case of pork; also dislike taste and price	Need for convenience overrules distaste for this product; highest usage rate	Prefer fresh and fatty cuts; lack refrigeration	Rank second to Puerto Ricans
Frozen Fruit Pie	Prefer sweets to be home-baked or made in local speciality bakeries	Crave sweets and this overcomes price and taste resistance	Lowest level of consumption for traditional reasons	Rank last in *per capita* consumption due to dislike of flavour
Instant Coffee	Favourable response but prefer tea to coffee	Do not drink much coffee	Diet favours instant coffee but economic position militates against its adoption. Rank last in purchase rates.	Prefer own special blends
Cake Mixes	Do not use much – reasons as for pie	Lead other groups in usage	Do not use much but use more than Jewish group	
Dehydrated Soups	Do not use	Use in large quantities	Use in limited amounts	Low consumption though high in usage versus non-usage

Source: Derived from M. Alexander, 'The significance of ethnic groups in marketing new-type packaged foods in Greater New York', *Proc. American Marketing Association*, 1959.

The precise reactions of the four subcultural groups to the convenience foods mentioned above are shown in Table 9.3; considerable differences from one to another are detectable and this means that differential marketing approaches may only be effective and profitable if the segments are sufficiently large to warrant economic production levels (where product or packaging differences are necessary) and where the competition from ethnic producers is not too strong (e.g. in the case of Jewish bakeries). If a distinct approach is made to each segment, there is the possibility of using in-store promotions and those involving samples and coupon-based offers to overcome resistance to new products. This is clearly possible in the case of Puerto Ricans, for instance, since this group reported difficulties in understanding instructions on packages.

Negro Consumers

American Negroes are probably the most over-surveyed subculture in
the marketing literature. Studies of this group have, nevertheless,
shown it to be highly important not only for marketing in practice but
in its implications for the academic study of consumption behaviour.
Many of the issues and areas of interest in this field were first
identified by Bauer, Cunningham and Wortzel in their study of the
'marketing dilemma of Negroes'.[22] Other noteworthy studies have
been carried out by Alexis,[23] and Rich;[24] the following discussion
draws in part on these sources.

Although average income levels and educational standards are
obvious differences between American whites and Negroes, there are
other important variations in the backgrounds and behaviour of these
groups. Even holding constant the effect of income, Negroes have very
different patterns of consumption from those of whites; they spend
less on food, housing, medical needs, car transport and insurance,
but more on clothing, home furnishings, other forms of transport and
savings. This suggests that the Negro whose income is the same as that
of a white person has a greater amount of discretionary income;
Negroes tend, therefore, to spend more on clothes, home furnishings
and alcoholic drinks than whites of similar income.

There are more basic differences than this, however, and these stem
in many ways from what Bauer *et al.* call the Negroes' basic marketing
dilemma: whether to live without the material trappings that
characterise white people's way of life or to strive to adopt middle
class American values and the economic goods and services which
accompany them. These authors also maintain that the Negro market
can be segmented into the high-strivers and the non-strivers and they
have re-analysed part of Rich's data for housewives in New York and
Cleveland to show the existence of two groups of women: those with
high levels of interest in fashion and those with low fashion interest.
In all income groups, Negro women showed greater fashion interest
(measured by the proportion in each income range interviewed who
expressed a fashion orientation) than white women. Again regardless of
income, the high-fashion Negroes tended to have more social activities
outside the home than comparable white housewives; for each income
range, the high-fashion Negro women were twice as likely to have social
activities outside their families than low-fashion Negro respondents.
This is not the case for white women in the sample.

The Negro women with high fashion-consciousness were assumed to
be the strivers after middle class values and status and significant

differences emerge from studies of their consumer behaviour as compared with that of the non-striving Negroes. Strivers are twice as likely as non-strivers to shop with others, for instance, and they are also likely to combine shopping trips with social affairs and entertainments such as lunching, going to the theatre and seeing friends.

Another theme that is apparent from studies of Negro consumers is their striving after status through the purchase of certain products and brands which they expect will confer prestige. Thus several writers have shown that *per capita* expenditure on alcohol tends to be rather higher for Negroes than for whites earning the same and Negro expenditure on Scotch whisky is disproportionally high compared with their numbers in the overall American population (see Table 9.4). Scotch is closely related to status in the eyes of many Negroes; Bauer *et al.* show that Negroes who perceive themselves as upwardly mobile socially (with reference to their fathers' social class positions) tend to report higher Scotch consumption than others. The authors note that these findings relate only to self-perceived status and not to present income.

Table 9.4 : Negro vs. White Scotch Consumption

	Proportion of U.S. Population	Proportion of Scotch consumption	Proportion who buy Scotch (families)
	%	%	%
Negroes	11	25	16.8
Whites and Other Non-Negroes	89	75	9.3

Source: Derived from R.A. Bauer *et al.*, 'The marketing dilemma of Negroes', *Journal of Marketing*, 29, 1965.

Data for Negroes' brand preferences with regard to Scotch also confirm that they are using whites as a reference group and that their perception of their status is such that they try to enhance their social position by selecting brands which are 'safe'. Some seventy-one per cent of the regular Negro Scotch drinkers in the sample reported that they had well-established brand preferences, while seventy-nine per cent claimed to name a specific brand of Scotch when ordering whisky in bars. Sixty-one per cent of habitual Negro drinkers replied affirmatively to the statement 'To obtain a good Scotch you have to order an old reliable brand' while only forty-nine per cent of white regular Scotch drinkers agreed with this. The evidence implies that

Negroes are unsure of their status and, rather than make a mistake, they confine their drinking to established brand. Even regular drinking and the expertise that accompanies it does not reduce their anxiety. A parallel is found in Negro women's buying behaviour with regard to fashion; the more fashion-conscious women reported difficulty in knowing what specific items to buy.

These data suggest that even within the 'northern, educated, urban' division of the overall Negro subculture, there is significant differentiation between the strivers after status and the non-strivers.

In a later review of the consumer behaviour of the American Negro, Bauer and Cunningham[25] draw attention to the increasing assimilation of Negroes into American life and the complexity of their buying behaviour. Kassarjian points out that none of the almost seven hundred television stations in the U.S.A. is owned by Negroes, and that only thirteen radio stations are Negro-owned (though over one hundred others are programmed by Negroes). Thus the Negro is 'locked into a practically all-white media world' but, even so, about two-thirds of Negroes listen to such stations and eighty-five per cent read some Negro periodicals.[26] Thus the Negro is part of a subculture which is readily accessible to the advertiser.

Relative Deprivation and Subcultures

A key to the behaviour of some subcultures is to be found in the concept of relative deprivation which is concerned with people's attitudes to social inequalities that reflect their own positions within the socio-economic hierarchy. Feelings of relative deprivation often stem from the adoption of a more privileged group as a reference point. It does not depend so much on absolute deprivation but on an individual's perception of his status or privileges in relation to those of another group in society. In fact, relative deprivation may not be an active influence on behaviour until the differences between the less privileged and the more privileged begin to narrow.

Runciman,[27] who originated the analysis of relative deprivation in connection with reference group behaviour, gives the following example of its operation: when few manual workers' children were in secondary education, not many working class families adopted such children as a reference group, but when this group of children increased in size, 'more working class families began to feel relatively deprived of education and of the status ..... associated with it'.

While the concept of relative deprivation has considerable relevance to the behaviour of social classes – middle classes as well as working classes, for 'many people at the bottom of society are less resentful of the system and many nearer the top are more so, than their actual position appears to warrant' — it is also of special significance in the context of subcultures, particularly where previously disprivileged subgroups begin to achieve some of the status and possessions they have hitherto lacked. Commenting on the composition of America's lower middle class, Warner[28] wrote 'Some of the more successful members of ethnic groups, such as Italians, Irish, French-Canadians, have reached this level. Only a few members of these cultural minorities have gone beyond it; none of them has reached the old-family level.'

It is probable that some of the behaviour of the 'striving' Negroes and other ethnic and class-based minorities can be understood in terms of the relative deprivation they perceive and that as the socio-economic position of subgroups in the U.S.A. and Britain becomes more favourable, at least for some members of these subcultures, the desires of other subculture members to enjoy a higher standard of living will increase dramatically. The results of this may not be seen in the market-place alone but also in the work-place where demands for higher pay and greater instrumental orientation to work may be felt; the 'embourgeoisement thesis' may then require further attention.

The Poor as a Subculture

Social class is frequently highly correlated with other characteristics of subcultures — many people who belong to the poorer sections of American and British societies are also members of ethnic subcultures, for instance. The poorer groups of consumers have been extensively studied in several cultures and have some common characteristics.

We have already seen that poor consumers in both the United States and Turkey tend to use small, local shops to satisfy their food requirements. Such customers also perceive themselves as belonging to their immediate neighbourhoods rather than to the city or region as a whole; their pattern of relationships with others shows that they inhabit closely knit communities and lack friends in places other than their home area. Additionally, 'the ghetto food shoppers are less psychologically mobile, less active, and more inhibited in their behaviour than their non-ghetto counterparts'.[29]

There is also evidence that poorer consumers pay more for their food than others, partly because the independent neighbourhood shops which they choose charge higher prices[30] and partly because the larger chain stores which have lower prices are inaccessible to them.[31] Further, modes of transportation used on shopping trips vary significantly for poor sections of the community compared with wealthier consumers; in a study of New Haven in the United States, middle-income groups were found to use either private cars (ninety-five per cent did so) or to walk to the shops (five per cent), while low-income consumers used cars much less (fifty-one per cent), their feet much more (forty-two per cent) and seven per cent went by public transport.[32] The average distance travelled by the middle-income customers were almost twice that travelled by the poorer buyers.

However, the evidence provided by the consumers' perceptions of their buying experience leads to the conclusion that the poor pay more because they purchase small sizes of many food products more frequently than the middle-income group. They appear to do so for reasons of limited food-related outlay and limited storage space. Some seventy-two per cent of the low-income respondents thought that larger packets were more economical while only sixty-four per cent of the middle-income buyers thought that this was true.

There is also reason to believe that poor consumers devote less time and expense to the search and evaluation phase of the buying process than higher-income consumers but this is an area that requires further investigation.[33] Other facets of this subculture's behaviour on which more information is needed are (i) the value ascribed to time spent on purchase activity especially with respect to the availability of various modes of transportation, (ii) comparison of the prices of various product and pack sizes (perhaps unit pricing practices lead to more 'rational' decision making among poorer consumers), (iii) the brand preference of poor versus wealthier customers, and (iv) the patterns of buying associated with non-food items.

Other Subgroups

Regional subcultures are also of use to marketing management although practical information about them usually refers to single aspects of their purchase behaviour rather than their overall way of life. For example, the penetration rates for several domestic appliances (washing machines, refrigerators, cookers and vacuum cleaners) vary from region to region in Britain[34] while in the United States consumers have been known to show marked preferences for brown eggs in Boston and for white eggs in New York.[35] Some advertising, however, does stress regional differences in styles of living; beer advertisements, for instance, stress Britain's regional accents and the local customs of people in the regions as well as reflecting a masculine appeal (which is often linked with the regional character of the people or brew — one beer is 'Brewed for the men of the Midlands', another 'for the men of the North').

Religion also exerts an influence on buying through the subcultures based upon it. Jewish subcultures have clear-cut dietary requirements and some Christian sects also specify the types of food and drink their members should consume. Companies which exploit these preferences can often make use of the publications and other media of particular religious organisations.

Another group — teenagers — do not constitute a subculture in the strict sense of the definition given above but to the extent that young adults exhibit a unique life-style they may act in a manner similar to that of other subcultures. The teenage market in Britain is now worth well in excess of the nearly £600 million spent by young women alone in 1970.[36] But the breakdown of this total shows some interesting patterns of consumer choice. About £150 million was spent on clothes, of which almost a fifth went on tights and other hose. Some £40 million was spent on cigarettes and £10 million on alcoholic drinks. Inflation since then has undoubtedly pushed these figures much higher and new measures of this market are, nowadays, out of date even before they are published.

The American teenage market is worth some $24 billion per year and Walters[37] suggests that this figure, for 'observed business', may represent only one quarter of the total buying influence of teenagers. Most Americans between the ages of sixteen and twenty-one are in college (about three-quarters of them) and there their principal buying habits involve clothing, furnishings, books and recreation. The modal age for girls getting married is eighteen and young families have several peculiar needs based on their stage in the family life cycle. The twenty-seven million teens in the U.S.A. constitute a segment of the population which is growing at a rate three times as fast as that of the populace as a whole.

Older individuals also form a sort of subculture.[38] In 1971 the U.S.A. had over seven million families whose heads were over sixty-five and by 1985 there will be twenty-five million people older than that. Senior citizens have special needs and spend a high proportion of their income on health products, smaller houses, insurance, recreation and services but less on clothes and travel.

Marketing Management, Cultures and Subcultures

Most of the lessons to be learned from the study of culture have been brought out in the above discussions. Many of them refer to constraints and negatives (the avoidance of certain colours, and so on) but there is a special advantage to be gained from incorporating cultural symbolisms or artifacts into the appeal to consumers. Several American products are promoted in Britain as though they were indispensable elements of the British way of life (e.g. chewing gum).

A fascinating study of American car salesmen shows that they treat customers very differently depending on the buyer's race, sex and dress.[39] Wise has shown that the salesmen were likely to react differently in one or more of three ways: the price they quoted, the treatment of the customer as a person, and a combination of these. Being well dressed did not help potential buyers to obtain lower price quotations whether they were black or white, but a poorly dressed black male was usually offered prices which were significantly higher than those proposed to both a well dressed black male and a poorly dressed white male. Well dressed Oriental men, however, were offered prices even higher than those offered poorly dressed black men.

Women were given better overall treatment than men to a very marked extent; but poorly dressed customers received worse treatment than others regardless of colour or sex. The author of the study states that it is natural that car salesmen will tend to evaluate prospective buyers on the basis of their physical characteristics. Nevertheless, there is always a possibility in this type of situation that sales will be lost simply because sales people react towards members of minority sub-cultures on the basis of stereotyped patterns of behaviour and speech. Many writers have commented on American firms which have lost sales because of discriminatory or prejudicial attitudes on the part of their salesmen — particularly where they have used disparaging nicknames such as 'Mack' or 'Joey'.

Britain contains several large subcultural groups whose consumer behaviour is different from that of the general population. Jewish groups can be found in London and Manchester which are large enough to support differential marketing approaches, and recently there have been large numbers of Indian, West Indian and Pakistani immigrants entering cities in the Midlands and North as well as the two main conurbations. With some exceptions, very many firms seem to show little specific interest in these subcultures. This attitude stems in part from the fact that the groups themselves may often make their own manufacturing and marketing arrangements and that their consumers prefer ethnically produced goods and services. There is also a tendency for firms to neglect obvious possibilities, however, and Chisnall[40] singles out those airline companies which have missed out on the opportunity of promoting holiday travel to the birthplaces of Britain's new racial groups.

The understanding of cultures and subcultures should be an integral part of the marketing and exporting expertise of consumer-orientated firms and it may be as a result of Britain's past worldwide industrial and economic success that some companies have neglected this area. There are signs, despite this, that some firms are hitting back and are becoming increasingly aware of the constraints and opportunities offered by cultural differences between consumers. [41, 42]

Summary

Culture adds another dimension to the study of consumer behaviour taking us beyond the individual and his social system. The concept refers to all those symbols, artifacts and behaviour patterns which are passed on socially (rather than physically) from one generation to the next. It includes cognitive elements, beliefs, values and norms, signs and non-normative behaviour. Although there are wide differences from one culture to another, there are certain cultural universals, items such as mourning and incest taboos, which are found in all known cultures. Subcultures are groups within society which reflect the basic structure of the overall society in which they occur but which have a different life-style which may be based on religion, race, region or class.

Perception varies from culture to culture and with it the reactions of consumers to products and to the symbolic representations of products. Many examples could be given of products which, although successful in their originating culture, have failed in others. Sometimes products fail because they are packaged in materials bearing colours which have connotations that are disapproved in a given society. Some anthropologists have pointed this out and have claimed that marketing should incorporate more concepts and techniques which are native to anthropology. Apart from certain applications, however, the contribution which anthropology can make has been exaggerated and is of relatively limited importance.

Cross-cultural comparisons show some similarities between family decision making on both sides of the Atlantic and between poorer consumers in the U.S.A. and Turkey. This remains, however, an area which would benefit from much more research. Ethnic subcultures are important to marketers, especially the American Negro subculture which appears to be assimilating slowly into the overall U.S. society and whose members have conflicting self-images. They seek status by buying established brands and experience anxiety about their buying. Teenage, regional and religious groups also show differential patterns of consumer behaviour and may justify a segmented marketing approach. Poor people, whose behaviour is partly explained by the concept of relative deprivation, also constitute a separate cultural group; they have special shopping habits but appear to pay more for their food requirements than others.

Marketing managers can benefit by avoiding clashes with foreign cultures and by shaping their products and promotions to fit in with the cultural imperatives of other cultures to which they are directed.

Notes

1. E.B. Tylor, *Primitive Culture*, Brentano, 1924, p. 1.
2. H.M. Johnson, *Sociology*, Routledge and Kegan Paul, 1962, p. 82.
3. R. Linton, *The Cultural Background of Personality*, Appleton-Century, 1945.
4. G.P. Murdock, 'Uniformities in culture', *American Sociological Review*, 5, 1940.
5. O.K. Moore and D.J. Lewis, 'Learning theory and culture', *Psychological Review*, 59, 1952.
6. Johnson, *Sociology*, pp. 86-95.
7. S.K. Langer, *Philosophy in a New Key: A Study in the Symbolism of Reason, Rite, and Art*, Harvard University Press, 1942, pp. 45-6 (cited by Johnson, op. cit.)
8. G.P. Murdock, 'The common denominator of cultures', in R. Linton (ed.), *The Science of Man in the World of Crisis*, Columbia University Press, 1945.
9. J.H. Myers and W.H. Reynolds, *Consumer Behaviour and Marketing Management*, Houghton Mifflin, 1967, p. 223.
10. G.R. Foxall and A.V. Seaton, 'Suggested developments for the sociology of consumption', unpublished paper, Department of Agricultural Marketing, Newcastle University, 1976.
11. D. Krech and R.S. Crutchfield, *The Individual and Society*, McGraw-Hill, 1948.
12. Johnson, *Sociology*, pp. 106-8.
13. J.D. McConnell, 'The economics of behavioural factors on the multinational corporation', *Proc. American Marketing Association*, 1971.
14. A. Thorncroft, 'When U.S. products fail in Britain', *Marketing*, May 1970
15. J.R.G. Jenkins, *Marketing and Customer Behaviour*, Pergamon, 1972, p. 62.
16. H.H. Kassarjian and T.S. Robertson, *Perspectives in Consumer Behaviour*, Scott Foresman, 1973, p. 453.
17. C. Winick, 'Anthropology's contributions to marketing', *Journal of Marketing*, 25, 1961.
18. D.J. Hempel, 'Family buying decisions: a cross-cultural perspective', *Journal of Marketing Research*, 11, 1974.
19. E. Kaynak, 'Shopping practices for food – some cross-cultural comparisons', *Proc. Marketing Education Group of the U.K.*, July 1976.
20. Myers and Reynolds, *Consumer Behaviour*, p. 223.
21. M. Alexander, 'The significance of ethnic groups in marketing new-type packaged foods in Greater New York', *Proc. American Marketing Association*, 1959.

22. R.A. Bauer *et al.*, 'The marketing dilemma of Negroes', *Journal of Marketing*, 29, 1965.

23. M. Alexis, 'Some Negro-white differences in consumption', *American Journal of Economics and Sociology*, 21, 1962.

24. S.U. Rich, *Shopping Behaviour of Department Store Customers*, Harvard University, 1963.

25. R.A. Bauer and S.M. Cunningham, 'The Negro Market', *Journal of Advertising Research*, 10, 1970.

26. W.M. Kassarjian, 'The mass media and America's black citizen', *Journalism Quarterly*, Summer 1973.

27. W.G. Runciman, *Relative Deprivation and Social Justice*, Routledge and Kegan Paul, 1966, pp. 95-6.

28. L.W. Warner, *Social Class in America*, Harper and Row, 1960.

29. Kaynak, 'Shopping practices for food'.

30. R. Alcaly and A. Klevorick, 'Food prices in relation to income level in New York City', *Journal of Business*, 44, 1971.

31. D.E. Sexton, 'Comparing the cost of food to blacks and to whites', *Journal of Marketing*, 35, 1971.

32. H. Kunreuther, 'Why the poor pay more for food', *Journal of Business*, 46, 1973.

33. Ibid., pp. 379-80.

34. D.A. Brown, *et al.*, 'Improving the sales forecast for consumer durables', *Journal of Marketing Research*, 2, 1965.

35. Jenkins, *Marketing and Customer Behaviour*, p. 65.

36. P.M. Chisnall, *Marketing: A Behavioural Analysis*, McGraw-Hill, 1975, p. 99 (citing an IPC survey).

37. C.G. Walters, *Consumer Behaviour: Theory and Practice*, Irwin, 1974, pp. 353-5.

38. Ibid., pp. 355-6.

39. G.L. Wise, 'Differential pricing and treatment by new-car salesmen: the effect of the prospect's race, sex, and dress', *Journal of Business*, 47, 1974.

40. P.M. Chisnall, 'Some cultural aspects of ethnic air travel', *Proc. Marketing Education Group of the U.K.*, 1976.

41. See Engel *et al*, *Consumer Behaviour*, Dryden Press, 1978, Chapter 4.

42. J. Piper, 'The affluent over-fifties', *Marketing*, July 1977; J. Piper, Britain's ethnic markets', *Marketing*, January 1977; C. Nuttall and S. Morris, 'Spending by T.V. regions', *Marketing*, August 1977.

10 INTEGRATION AND APPLICATION

Chapters 2 to 9 have dealt separately with a number of behavioural science concepts by describing and evaluating them individually in terms of their ability to contribute to the analysis of consumer behaviour. Consumer research is usually undertaken with a view to the improvement of practical decision making, particularly in the sphere of marketing management, and it is seldom the case that a single variable is able to supply all of the answers that business executives require. Market development programmes and the planning and introduction of new products demand complex analyses of the dynamics of consumer choice and thus entail the understanding, measurement and prediction of numerous variables and the relationships which exist between them. Application of the behavioural sciences in marketing demands the integration of research results gathered in a wide range of investigations; and, the more we attempt to relate consumer behaviour to the practical concerns of management, the greater is our need of an overall comprehension of the activities of customers which impinge on executive decisions.

Two approaches to integration and application are explored in this concluding chapter. The approach of academics to the problem of integration has frequently involved the construction of formal models of consumers' decision-making processes: these models, which were briefly mentioned in the introductory chapter, are here examined in greater detail and some of their merits and demerits are discussed. The second approach involves the comparison and appraisal of those findings which are relevant to a specific marketing problem (such as the need to make use of a particular phenomenon like consumer loyalty) or which elucidate an area of public concern (for instance, the extent to which advertising is capable of persuading customers against their own better judgement). In order to illustrate this more pragmatic approach to the use of the behavioural sciences in marketing, each of these examples is also examined below.

Models of Consumer Decision Making

Any set of statements which identify and relate the concepts and constructs in terms of which consumer behaviour may be described and, more importantly, explained and predicted may be referred to as a model of the consumer choice process. Formal models have several advantages for consumer researchers, particularly those engaged in academic investigations. For example, models are capable of drawing together, integrating and interrelating research results which have been collected in a variety of contexts and of which the separate explanatory power is limited. The successful construction of a model of consumer behaviour can also assist in the forecasting of aggregate consumer demand and in the prediction of the buying decisions that will be made by specific segments of heterogeneous markets. Furthermore, the formal representation of our knowledge about consumer decision making may suggest hitherto-untested relationships between concepts and variables and this may serve to stimulate and guide further empirical investigation; finally, the use of models has pedagogical advantages in that it allows knowledge to be structured and simplifies explanation.[1]

In order to judge how far these putative advantages of consumer behaviour models have in fact been translated into reality by academic researchers, it is useful to examine specific examples of model building which have had a considerable impact on the development of consumer behaviour as a discipline in its own right. The models presented by Nicosia[2] and Howard and Sheth[3] are especially appropriate in this context since they have received considerable attention from marketing educators and practitioners.

Nicosia considers the manner in which a consumer reacts to the introduction of a new product by depicting the sequence of decisions involved in the potential buyer's becoming aware of the novel good, searching for alternative means of satisfying his wants and evaluating them, together with the newly introduced item. The model, which is presented as a flow diagram, also includes the act of purchase itself, the consumer's experience of the use of the product and the feedback which the firm receives as a result of its monitoring purchase behaviour in the market-place. In many respects, this is a comparatively simple model to understand and is entirely consistent with the account of the buying process which was presented in the introduction to this book.

In the first stage of the decision sequence (which Nicosia calls 'Field One: From the Source of a Message to the Consumer's Attitude') the attributes of the firm and of the consumer are understood to determine the advertiser's promotional message and its reception and comprehension by the potential buyer as it permeates his perceptual and predispositional subfield. In the second stage ('Field Two: Search for, and Evaluation of, Means-Ends Relations') the consumer's attitude towards the product is assumed to determine the nature of his search and evaluation behaviour as he identifies and appraises alternative products; this process ends when the consumer reaches a state of motivation in which he desires to purchase the item. Field Three ('The Act of Purchase') leads on to the storage and/or consumption of the product, the consumer's subjective judgement of its value and the subsequent modification of his attitude towards the product. The feedback of consequential market intelligence to the firm completes the model (Field Four).

Howard and Sheth's model is considerably more elaborate than this; Lunn[4] refers to it as 'by far the most thorough, comprehensive and well-articulated model of the consumer published to date'. Three classes of input are assumed to impinge upon the consumer: *significative inputs* are such factors as quality, price, distinctiveness, service and availability as they influence the consumer directly through the attributes of the product; *symbolic inputs* are the same factors as they affect the consumer indirectly through their portrayal in the mass media and by salesmen; finally, *social inputs* include family, reference group and social class influences. Any of these variables acting on the potential buyer may make him aware of new knowledge and, by evoking a state of confusion or, as the authors term it, *stimulus ambiguity*, lead him to search for further information about the product in question. Stimulus ambiguity occurs within the context of the consumer's perceptual biases and general psychological make-up. The consumer's motives, attitudes and comprehension of the brand in question affect his degree of confidence in the product, his intentions to buy, and his actual purchase behaviour. The extent to which the buyer is satisfied with his purchase feeds back as modifying information which affects his attitudes, confidence and purchase intentions.[5]

It is undeniable that these models have assisted academic research by making possible the integration of knowledge and by encouraging empirical investigations which might otherwise not have taken place or which would have had to be preceded by lengthy exploratory work. Further, only a cursory account of each of the models mentioned has been possible here and the reader is recommended to examine the original accounts before judging finally their relevance to practical marketing decision making. Nevertheless, it is clear that, by their very nature, formal models of the consumer choice process of the type under consideration are unlikely to enhance managerial decision making generally. Models are necessarily abstractions from reality; the simplifying assumptions on which they are inevitably based make them poor guides to the 'real world' and thus render them of very limited value to the practical marketing executive and commercial researcher. The models which have been presented are also extremely difficult to subject to empirical testing and, where testing has taken place, the results have been equivocal.[6] The relationships between the variables which are included in a given model frequently seem arbitrary, indicating that the models could be fundamentally restructured if rather different weightings were accorded to one or other of the many factors which are known to influence actual consumer decisions. There is a serious paucity of factual data to verify the social and psychological relationships posited by Nicosia, Howard, Sheth and others;[7] all of the models of this type fail to incorporate more than a handful of empirical results and relationships; most give scant attention to social and environmental factors; and, finally, all preclude a holistic or Gestalt approach to the behaviour of consumers. The search for integrative and practical views of consumer behaviour cannot be concluded at this stage and it is valuable to assess the behavioural approach to consumer activity by examining the ways in which our knowledge of patterns of buyer behaviour can lead to specific marketing policies and strategies.

Consumer Loyalty

Competitive marketing systems emphasise the amount of choice which is available to consumers. Techniques which have the objective of persuading buyers to switch brands, try new products or visit recently opened or revamped stores are prominent in such economies. As a result, it can be difficult to observe and predict stable patterns of consumer behaviour and buying sometimes appears superficially to be a random process.

Yet an intriguing facet of purchase behaviour is presented by the tendency of many customers to be loyal to a particular brand or store. Marketing researchers have, of course, been long aware of this and the concept of consumer loyalty has become the subject of sophisticated definitions and measurement. One rather elaborate definition of brand loyalty depicts it as 'the preferential, attitudinal and behavioural response to one or more brands in a product category expressed over a period of time by a consumer'.[8] But the idea of consumer loyalty is usually understood by marketing managers more simply as the extent to which buyers repeatedly select a favourite brand or make use of a specific store.

Understood in this way, the phenomenon of consumer loyalty offers a valuable approach to some of the problems faced by marketing managers. Before spelling out the aspects of consumer loyalty to which the practitioner should be alert, however, it is necessary to examine the meanings of loyalty and the social and psychological profile of the loyal consumer.

Meanings of Loyalty

Some of the pioneering research into consumer loyalty was carried out in the 1950s by R.H. Brown, who posed the exploratory question of whether brand loyalty was fiction or fact.[9] He concluded, on the basis of a wide range of product tests, that loyalty was a reality but he distinguished four possible types of consumer behaviour, each of which involved a different degree of loyalty or none at all.

Undivided loyalty, in which a consumer bought the same brand on every occasion without exception, was contrasted with *divided loyalty* where two similar brands were purchased alternately. Consumers might also show *unstable loyalty* to some brands as, for example, when they purchased brands A and B in the sequence A A A B B B. Finally some consumers chose brands randomly and were said to show *no loyalty*. Brown's analysis of consumer behaviour for specific products showed that undivided loyalty characterised the markets for toothpaste, coffee, flour, shampoo and headache remedies. He discovered unstable loyalty among orange juice buyers but no loyalty was apparent in the cases of margarine, cereals and soap. Nevertheless, his overall conclusion was that most buyers tend to choose a favourite brand or group of brands.

Various studies have been concerned with the extent and forms of brand loyalty but some recent evidence emerges from a Nielsen[10] survey which was primarily concerned with distribution. Shoppers were asked as they left supermarkets whether they had been successful in obtaining the brands they had wanted to buy. One in nine respondents (2,552 out of 22,000) had in fact been unable to buy their favourite brand because of its non-availability. What did they do instead? Just over a third had bought a substitute while the vast majority preferred to try again later or to obtain their favoured brand elsewhere.

These results, which are presented more fully in Table 10.1, indicate the importance of consumers' brand preferences for distribution planning. Whilst they do not provide evidence of continuing brand loyalty, they show that many customers are willing to experience delay and inconvenience in order to obtain their desired brands.

Store loyalty, which has been extensively reviewed by Charlton,[11] is also a common pattern of consumer behaviour. In most weeks, more than four-fifths of British housewives buy all of their groceries at one

Table 10.1 : Reactions to Out-of-Stock Situation

	All Products	Food For later use	For immediate use	Non-food
	%	%	%	%
Bought Substitute	35	32	48	26
different size/ same brand	5	5	7	2
different brand/ same category	25	22	35	22
other product	5	5	6	2
Did Not Buy	65	68	52	74
intention :				
to buy later	26	23	21	33
to buy elsewhere	39	45	31	41

Source: Nielsen Researcher, No. 3, 1975.

or two shops and their store preferences often display considerable continuity and stability. Just as there are degrees of brand loyalty, so store loyalty shows variations among different groups of consumers. In an American survey,[12] families were ranked according to the amount of loyalty each showed. The most loyal family spent over nine-tenths of its grocery budget at its favourite food store while the least loyal family spent under a fifth at its favourite shop. The average for all families was about one half (see Table 10.2).

Table 10.2 : Loyalty to Six Favourite Stores

Store	% of Total Food Purchases
First favourite	49
Second favourite	21
Third favourite	10
Fourth favourite	6
Fifth favourite	4
Sixth favourite	3

Source: R.M. Cunningham, 'Customer loyalty to store and brand', *Harvard Business Review*, November 1962.

Correlates of Loyalty

Descriptive accounts of the varied patterns of consumer loyalty could easily be multiplied. But more important than these are the social and psychological characteristics which are typical of loyal customers. If we can identify these 'behavioural correlates' of loyalty, it should be easier to use the existence of consumer loyalty as the basis for marketing policies and strategies — for example, in market segmentation. Although most customers exhibit loyalty to some extent and in some contexts, we need to know more than this about the phenomenon of loyalty, if it is to be more than an abstract concept. In identifying the correlates of brand and store loyalty we are really asking 'What kind of consumer is loyal?' with the expectation that this knowledge can be incorporated into marketing practice.

While the precise *causes* of loyalty among consumers are still largely unknown, we do know something of the areas of human behaviour which are connected positively or negatively with loyalty (these are summarised in Table 10.3). A link between the two forms of loyalty which have been discussed is found in the observation that customers who are brand loyal tend also to be loyal to the places where they shop. Part of the reason for this stems from the fact that no single shop can normally stock every available brand and so anyone who restricts the number of shops visited automatically reduces the range of brands they are likely to buy. 'Shopping proneness', which is a measure of the number of shops visited, bears this out, since the housewives who are not shopping prone tend to exhibit a high level of store loyalty (by definition almost) and are also brand loyal.[13]

Table 10.3 : Summary of Research Findings on Consumer Loyalty and its Correlates

	Related	*Unrelated*	*Ambiguous*
Brand Loyalty	Store loyalty Sociability Self-confidence Thrift Household size Shopping proneness Cohesiveness Type of product	Social, demographic and psychological factors generally Social class Sex Intelligence Marital status	Age Inter-purchase time Amount purchased
Store	Education Social class Brand loyalty Market share of store Type of store	Social and psychological factors generally Amount spent	

Social interaction is also closely associated with loyalty according to some researchers. The more the housewife socialises with her neighbours, the more likely she is to be brand loyal. Further, the more cohesive the housewife's informal social group, the more likely she is to buy the same brand as the group's leader.[14] Personal characteristics also affect loyalty in consumers and self-confidence in particular is an attribute of many housewives who are brand loyal. This effect seems to be confined to certain products, however. While it is well demonstrated in the case of coffee, it is not relevant to all purchase decisions.[15]

Care is obviously necessary in interpreting the results of survey research in this area. Some research findings plainly contradict others; notably, those dealing with such factors as the consumer's age, the time that elapses between purchases, and the amount purchased are ambiguous. Thus, while Coulson[16] reported that brand-loyal consumers were not different in age from non-loyal buyers, Day[17] concluded that the older customer was more likely to be brand loyal. The Nielsen survey which has already been mentioned lends support to the second view; it shows that, the older the customer, the more likely she is to refuse to buy anything at all if her favourite brand is out-of-stock.

Common sense suggests that the same brand is probably repurchased when the time between purchase acts is short and certainly this is a clear result of the work of Kuehn[18] which was concerned with frozen orange juice. But more recent research has failed to substantiate this pattern; for a wide range of food products, time makes no difference to the brand which is chosen.[19]

The prospect that heavy users of a product are more brand loyal than other purchasers has often been suggested. The empirical results are, however, contradictory. Kuehn's study of the orange juice market led him to the conclusion that heavy users tended to be brand loyal. There is also evidence from Day's work that buyers of convenience foods are loyal to one brand if they purchase large quantities of these items. Unfortunately, this relationship does not appear to be universally valid.[20] From a survey which was admittedly limited to three products — coffee, tea and ginger beer — Frank[21] and his colleagues concluded that loyalty was not significantly associated with heavy buying. The only conclusion which can be drawn from these various studies is that certain factors are related to consumer loyalty for some products but this effect is not proven.

A wide range of social and psychological variables has been employed in tests of brand loyalty but none appears to be a useful predictor of this aspect of consumer behaviour. Social class, which has a pervasive effect on so much consumer choice activity, is not relevant here; nor are sex, intelligence, marital status, family size or education.[22]

Many basic behavioural factors are unconnected with store loyalty, too, but there are interesting exceptions, notably education and social class. Ennis and Paul[23] demonstrate that store loyalty is higher among housewives with a lower social class position and those whose education was completed at a relatively young age. Carman[24] argues on the basis of empirical research that non-loyal customers are those who have time to shop. The loyal housewife, on the other hand, 'is the busy woman who typically is working to help support a family' and this also suggests that there is an inverse relationship between store loyalty and social class membership. The implication is that the lower class housewife who works mainly for economic reasons has to form habits in order to economise on the time it takes her to shop. If this is so, it is understandable that she patronises the stores which make shopping easy and quick.

Two other factors deserve to be mentioned briefly. Shops which command a relatively large share of the total market in their area tend to enjoy the loyalty of more customers than do shops with smaller market shares. And, further, it appears that people are more loyal to multiple or chain stores than to either independent traders or shops with specialised markets such as butchers or greengrocers.

Applying the Concept

Discussion of consumer loyalty is dangerous if it gives the impression that all customers are loyal or that loyalty is a static attribute of some market segments. The reality is that loyalty is rarely if ever absolute — where loyalty occurs, it is more likely to be divided than undivided. This has important consequences for the application of the idea of loyalty in marketing management.

Attempts at making use of the concept of consumer loyalty frequently centre on market segmentation policies; the hope is that loyal customers may form a substantial market segment which will justify a specialised marketing approach. In fact, the evidence that this is possible is, to say the least, equivocal. Reynolds,[25] among others, has cast doubt on the crude assumption that consumers have an unchanging preference for a single brand or store. Rather, the evidence suggests that they 'select from an array of acceptable products' and that some apparent market segments may be based on no more than consumers buying at random. This does not rule out effective segmentation, of course, but it draws attention to the possibility of a manufacturer producing two or three similar brands which compete in the market-place but which ensure the firm against erratic changes in pattern of so-called loyalty.

Consumer behaviour can be a highly dynamic phenomenon. In some markets, where competitive pressures are especially strong, attitudes are also subject to frequent change. Table 10.4, which is derived from a study of the effects of three waves of advertising on buyers' attitudes and behaviour, shows clearly that customers' intentions and preferences with respect to purchase behaviour are frequently modified. Nearly three-quarters of the respondents changed their attitudes at least once during the three advertising campaigns and over a fifth tried new brands of products which ranged from analgesics to mouthwash, from hairspray to peanut butter.

Table 10.4 : Changes in Customers' Attitudes and Behaviour over Three Advertising Campaigns

	changed once	% of audience who changed twice	did not change
Attitudes	40	33	27
Behaviour	15	6	79

Source: A. Achenbaum, 'Advertising doesn't manipulate consumers', *Journal of Advertising Research*, April 1972.

Another aspect of consumer loyalty to which marketing managers should be alert is the possibility of its general decline as the effects of competitive forces, advertising, consumerism and changes in consumer preferences and sophistication become more widespread. In the mid-1950s, over half of the housewives interviewed in a survey of British consumers stated that they *always* used the same grocery shop. By the mid-1960s this proportion had dropped to less than one quarter. This is in spite of the tendency for there to be fewer shops available to the shopper as supermarkets replace independent grocery outlets.[26]

Summary and Practical Implications

Several recommendations for marketing management may be derived from this account of consumer loyalty.

1. The reality of consumer loyalty as an aspect of buying behaviour can

hide the fact that loyalty is rarely undivided and stable. The dynamic nature of consumer behaviour in a competitive economy stems from the large amount of choice available to customers and the social and psychological pressures to try whatever is new and whatever is being used by others. Thus, while measures of loyalty can be useful to the firm, they are essentially descriptions of a phenomenon that can change at any time.

2. The policy of marketing several similar and competing brands thus commends itself as a means of ensuring a measure of sales and profits stability for the firm when its customers switch brands. Even if a newly introduced brand 'cannibalises' the sales of more established brands, there can be an overall gain to the firm. Reynolds[27] provides the example of the Mustang which, despite its reduction of the sales of other Ford models, generated enough sales to become a great marketing success.

3. Alternatively, a policy of market segmentation might be considered. The success of such an approach depends, of course, on identifying brand/store-loyal users as a sufficiently large group to support differential production and/or marketing effort and it has to be admitted that this has proved a difficult proposition. Psychographic segmentation, especially when based on personality variables, has proved a notoriously difficult policy to implement. There are exceptions to this generalisation, however, such as the cold remedy market, which may be subdivided into those buyers who believe the remedy will work and those who think that they should take something but doubt its efficacy.[28] Specific examples based on consumer loyalty are more difficult to substantiate but supermarket sales in some areas reflect segmental buying as consumers select the store with the atmosphere, range of products and prices that suit them best.

4. Finally, it is as well to remember that many propositions about consumer loyalty have yet to be established through empirical research. Thus, our overall conclusion has to be 'handle with care': consumer loyalty is a potentially useful concept but requires sound research and planning before it can be successfully exploited. The ubiquitous need for marketing practice to be based firmly on research, for managers to be constantly in touch with their markets, is once again emphasised.

Advertising, Persuasion and Manipulation

Of all the functions of business, marketing receives the most criticism from all sections of the community. Within marketing, advertising comes in for the greatest amount of attack, though packaging runs a close second. Research workers in the marketing field, especially those concerned with consumer behaviour research, are often accused of trying to discover ways of manipulating customers.

It was pointed out in the first chapter of this book that nearly three-quarters of food products fall at the stage of consumer acceptance and, for many other product ranges, the figure for failures approximates ninety per cent. Further, a 1973 study of new product failures carried out by Nielsen[29] shows that some sixty-seven per cent of failures can be attributed to the product itself or its package and that advertising also accounts for about three per cent of failures. (The remaining thirty per cent are split evenly between trade non-acceptance and mistakes in pricing.) These figures hardly substantiate the impression that marketeers are able to control the behaviour of consumers in some sinister manner.

There is no doubt, of course, that marketing tries to persuade buyers but persuasion is perfectly legitimate in an open society and is preferable by far to its historical alternatives: military coercion or religious ignorance used as a political weapon. The figures which have been quoted also leave little doubt about the power of business to persuade. It has a long way to go before it is likely to be able to over-ride the power of the consumer in the market-place.

Nevertheless, the theme of this book, the application of the behavioural sciences to the analysis, understanding and prediction of consumer choice may give the impression that marketing management has at its command a virulent form of psychology or sociology which can be used against the best interests of the consumer. This view deserves closer attention.

Behavioural Science in Marketing

An eminent sociologist wrote recently of 'the near criminal — certainly amoral and frequently immoral — activities of salesmen whose techniques and acumen probably rest nowadays upon research which includes depth psychology and sociology' and which are 'sufficient to make anyone of good sense feel critical about accepting the uses of the human sciences unguardedly'.[30] His remarks contain two points worthy of note to anyone involved in advertising, selling and marketing: sales techniques are to be criticised because they are manipulative; and this manipulation is said to be based on methods devised by behavioural scientists. It is, indeed, true that advertising needs to be, and is, persuasive, and that advertising men take note of the social and psychological factors that influence consumers. But throwing these two facts together, as in this quotation, may well be more deceptive than the practices it seeks to condemn.

Thus criticised, we are justified in asking what is the evidence for the critics' claims? Have we really got the ultimate tools of consumer manipulation? Do the behavioural sciences themselves shed any light on the question of manipulation? Their criticism of advertising and other methods of sales stimulation are, of course, not new. The charge that such techniques are to a large extent manipulative has been made by economists and others for decades; they are well summarised in J.K. Galbraith's claims about the advertising industry. 'In everyday parlance', he says, 'this great machine, and the demanding and varied talents that it employs, are said to be engaged in selling goods. In less ambiguous language, it means that it is engaged in the management of those who buy goods'.[31] Let us consider in greater detail the ramifications of the critics' arguments.

Only a little thought is necessary to dispel the force of their criticism: for if advertising were capable of all the mind-bending feats attributed to it by its critics, it would probably have no critics. Advertising men, being unscrupulous of heart (another aspect of the image held by critics), would enjoy the constant adulation of a satisfied and unsuspecting public. Rather than being accused at every turn of influencing helpless consumers to lay out enormous sums of money against their better judgement, members of the advertising profession would be continually praised for their socially and educationally valuable contributions. For if they were as bereft of moral sense as is often supposed, they would by now have employed their assumed remarkable powers in the marketing of themselves, and no one outside their ranks could possibly become aware of it.

This picture of total manipulation in practice is, of course, pure fantasy. In a world where every advertisement competes with thousands of other attempts at persuasion, mind bending of this sort is impossible, even if the instruments of persuasion were available. Anyone who has tried to persuade others knows that consumers' attention is not simply there for the asking; and attention is only the beginning of a perceptual process which is fully capable of screening out unwanted messages at any stage. Furthermore, advertising men themselves appear to be among the most self-conscious and self-critical of professionals: a characteristic only befitting anyone so centrally involved in the communications process. Quite apart from the social and ethical considerations involved in misleading or deceptive communications, the advertising man is concerned about criticisms of his work simply in order that he may become a more proficient agent of communication.

Conflicting Interests

Yet he is faced with two conflicting interests. He has to convince clients and potential clients that his advertising works; and at the same time he has to assure public watchdogs and critics that it does not work too well. Both considerations are rendered complex by the apparent inability of anyone to appraise the economic effects of a given advertisement (except in a few relatively unimportant circumstances, e.g. mail order selling), let alone its social and psychological results. And who knows how advertising really works? Even a short perusal of the literature of advertising and marketing research indicates that many writers, having described the results of yet another empirical survey, find it incumbent on them to offer a new explanation or to modify dramatically old ones.

Critics may nevertheless argue that consumer researchers are employing psychological techniques to investigate the consumer's mind, to uncover people's subconscious motives and to exploit consumers' drives and desires, of which they themselves may be unaware. It is undeniable that there is a great interest in incorporating measures of consumers' behaviour in marketing communications. For all we know, there may be a group of unscrupulous paranoids who will not be happy until consumers are conditioned to react like Pavlov's dogs, rushing to the shops, mouths watering, at the faintest suggestion that they should buy. But let us keep our feet on the ground. The agencies claim that using psychology in marketing fulfils their desire to serve consumers. Whether or not this is taken at face value by critics, they should at least ask themselves what the actual results of using behavioural science techniques and concepts in advertising have been.

Nothing agitated advertising's critics as much as the announcement that *motivation research* — 'that set of miracle tools available to plumb the depths of the consumer's psyche in some mysterious way'[32] — was being employed in marketing. Enthusiasm about these techniques originated in the marketing profession itself, but was short-lived. Once the initial clamour had died down, marketing and advertising men admitted that motivation research had not achieved the breakthrough it had seemed to promise. One psychologist[33] referred to its 'intuitive, non-scientific and often far-fetched procedures and notions'. It was admitted that its methods were not necessarily valid or reliable[34], and that it really represented no more than an 'extension of classical market research techniques'.[35] The fact that it was not primarily concerned with motives was overlooked by many critics; but the damage had been done by zealous marketeers and advertisers. As was mentioned in Chapter 3, a recent survey of marketing practitioners revealed that motivation research has now 'passed its messianic phase. It has now been, or is being absorbed into the repertoire of more mature research practice.'[36]

Matching the *personality* characteristics of products with those of consumers appears on the surface as either a brilliant marketing idea or a devilishly cunning way of getting at unsuspecting buyers, depending on your point of view. Sadly, for both parties, it does not seem to work in practice. Attempts at correlating the personality traits and types of consumers with aspects of their buying behaviour and brand images have produced a mass of weak associations; often different studies of the same trait and product or brand have led to contradictory conclusions. At the most, only five or ten per cent of consumer behaviour is explicable in terms of personality factors, and that is hardly a useful starting point for the marketing manager, whether or not he is bent on manipulation.

The notion that people reject information or behaviour patterns which conflict with their current perceptions also promised some years ago to assist marketing decision making. Festinger's *cognitive dissonance* theory suggests yet another method of discovering what goes on in the 'black box' of the consumer's mind. Yet what has its applications to this area produced that is useful? Only the assertion that it is frequently necessary to reassure purchasers of expensive occasionally-bought items that they have made the right decision. This idea is based on the finding that car buyers tend to read advertisements relating to their chosen brand after the purchase has taken place, and even that has been questioned. No method of generating dissonance that leads to a purchase being made has been put forward to date.

Consumer Behaviour

The import of this is not that behavioural sciences in advertising and marketing are useless and should be scrapped. Not infrequently they have provided exploratory or confirmatory information which has helped ensure that consumers get what they want. They shed valuable light on the question of why consumers behave as they do. But they are far from perfect even for that purpose, let alone for allowing advertising men and others to override the free will of potential customers. However, it is also evident that it has often been the agencies' misplaced zeal for promising new techniques which has exacerbated the indignation of the critics.

Whatever their value as an aid to management decision making, the findings of behavioural research are of help in deciding just how much advertising may contribute to consumer manipulation. For example, in order to ascertain the effect of advertising on customers' attitudes, Achenbaum[37] obtained data on 2,000 consumers from an American advertising agency. His analysis of the information was presented to the Federal Trade Commission of the United States in order to clarify the position of advertising's role in a highly developed economy and was alluded to in the discussion of consumer loyalty.

The major results of the survey were these: between the first and second waves of advertising, fifty-three per cent of consumers changed their attitudes; another forty-eight per cent did so between the second and third waves. The magnitude of attitude change varied from forty-one per cent (in the case of a hairspray) to sixty-one per cent (a denture cleanser). Although there was a tendency for some consumers to be loyal to a particular brand, and for these buyers to have relatively fixed attitudes, there were always more people whose attitudes did not alter than whose opinions were stable.

Behaviour was found to vary consistently with attitudes but experience with products exerted a powerful influence on opinions and propensity to buy. Between the first and second waves, thirteen per cent of consumers switched brands; another twelve per cent did so between waves two and three. There was clear evidence that most consumers were willing to try new brands rather than remain slavishly loyal to one throughout their lives. The author concluded: 'Consumers' attitudes vary as widely and frequently as does purchase behaviour. Consumers rarely stick to any one brand. If advertising affects their attitudes, it hardly mesmerises them.'

Clearly, the application of the behavioural sciences to advertising and marketing has not resulted in the accumulation of a set of diabolical instruments which allow advertising men to circumvent the normal mental processes of consumers. Rather, what we have learned of consumer behaviour through these sciences suggests that advertising is far from being manipulative.

A Conclusion

As the above survey shows, the investigation of consumer behaviour is one of the most promising fields of endeavour for those who manage commercial organisations or are professionally concerned with consumer education and protection. Since this book is subtitled *A Practical Guide*, it must be concluded that for the marketing practitioner the most fruitful source of applicable insights into consumer decision making is bound to be the careful and critical examination of research results in the context of particular marketing problems and opportunities; that is, the second approach which has been pursued in this chapter. While this should not lead to the conclusion that the more academic approach is invalid, it serves as a reminder to marketing researchers generally that their work should not exclude problem-orientated approaches or seek theoretical integration for its own sake. The new spirit of self-criticism which is slowly pervading the consumer research community[38] and the willingness to suggest and try out new research methodologies[39] provide considerable hope that the development of consumer research programmes in colleges and universities will indeed support and facilitate managerial decision making and consumer welfare.

Notes

1. C.G. Walters, *Consumer Behavior: Theory and Practice*, Irwin, 1974, Chapter 3.

2. F.M. Nicosia, *Consumer Decision Processes*, Prentice-Hall, 1966.

3. J.A. Howard and J.N. Sheth, *The Theory of Buyer Behaviour*, Wiley, 1969.

4. J.A. Lunn, 'A review of consumer decision process models', in P. Doyle *et al.* (eds), *Analytical Marketing Management*, Harper and Row, 1974.

5. See Walter, op. cit., pp. 56-8.

6. U.J. Farley and L.W. Ring, ' "Empirical" specification of a buyer behaviour model', *Journal of Marketing Research*, 11, 1974.

7. M. Tuck, *How Do We Choose?* Methuen, 1976.

8. J.F. Engel *et al.*, *Consumer Behavior*, Dryden Press, 1978, p. 552.

9. R.H. Brown, 'Brand loyalty — fact or fiction?' *Advertising Age*, 24, 1953.

10. *Nielsen Researcher*, No. 3, 1975.

11. P. Charlton, 'A Review of shop loyalty', *Journal of the Market Research Society*, 15, 1, 1973.

12. R.M. Cunningham, 'Customer loyalty to store and brand', *Harvard Business Review*, 40, 6, 1962.

13. J. Carman, 'Correlates of brand loyalty', *Journal of Marketing Research*, 6, 1, 1970.

14. J.E. Stafford, 'Effect of group influences on consumer brand preferences', *Journal of Marketing Research*, 4, 1, 1968.

15.   R.P. Brody and S.M. Cunningham, 'Personality variables and the consumer decision process', *Journal of Marketing Research*, 4, 1, 1968.

16.   J.S. Coulson, 'Buying decisions within the family', in J. Newman (ed.), *On Knowing the Consumer*, Wiley, 1966.

17.   G.S. Day, 'A two-dimensional concept of brand loyalty', *Journal of Advertising Research*, 9, 3, 1969.

18.   A. Kuehn, 'Consumer brand choice as a learning process', *Journal of Advertising Research*, 2, 2, 1962.

19.   J.M. Carman, 'Brand switching and linear learning models', *Journal of Advertising Research*, 6, 2, 1966.

20.   D.G. Morrison, 'Inter-purchase time and brand loyalty', *Journal of Marketing Research*, 2, 3, 1966.

21.   R.E. Frank *et al.*, 'Purchasing behavior and personal attributes', *Journal of Advertising Research*, 9, 4, 1969.

22.   R.E. Frank, 'Correlates of buying behavior for grocery products', *Journal of Marketing*, 31, 3, 1967.

23.   B.M. Ennis and G.W. Paul, Store loyalty as a basis for market segmentation', *Journal of Retailing*, Fall 1970.

24.   Carman, op. cit., reference 19.

25.   W.R. Reynolds, 'More sense about market segmentation', *Harvard Business Review*, 43, 5, 1965.

26.   Charlton, 'A review of shop loyalty'.

27.   Reynolds, 'More sense about market segmentation'.

28.   G. Wills, 'Market segmentation', in T. Kempner (ed.), *A Handbook of Management*, Penguin Books, 1976.

29.   Anon., 'Test marketing reduces risks', *Nielsen Researcher*, No. 1, 1973, p. 10.

30.   R. Fletcher, *The Making of Sociology*, Vol. 1, Michael Joseph, 1971, p. 6

31.   J.K. Galbraith, *The New Industrial State*, Penguin Books, 1967, p. 320.

32.   J.F. Engel *et al.*, *Consumer Behavior*, Dryden Press, 1978.

33.   H.J. Eysenck, 'Organisation, nature and measurement of attitudes', in *Attitude Scaling*, Market Research Society, 1960, p. 13.

34.   S.H. Britt, 'Four hazards of motivation research', *Printers' Ink*, June 1955, p. 40.

35.   H. Henry, *Perspectives in Management, Marketing and Research*, Crosby Lockwood, 1971, p. 323.

36.   L. Collins and C. Montgomery, 'Whatever happened to motivation research? End of the messianic hope', *Journal of the Market Research Society*, 12, 1, 1970.

37.   A.A. Achenbaum, 'Advertising doesn't manipulate consumers', *Journal of Advertising Research*, 12, 2, 1972.

38.   J. Jacoby, 'Consumer research: a state of the art review', *Journal of Marketing*, 42, 1978.

39.   M. Christopher, 'Marketing research and the real world', *European Research*, May 1978.

A GUIDE TO FURTHER STUDY

The most comprehensive text avilable is Engel, Blackwell and Kollat's *Consumer Behaviour* (3rd edition, Dryden Press, 1978) which cites numerous studies in each of the areas covered in this book. Engel *et al.* also present an original model of consumer decision making which they have amended with each new edition of their text and which has proved useful to marketing educators. Another valuable text is Walter's *Consumer Behaviour* (3rd edition, Irwin, 1978). Among the many introductory texts on the market, Myers and Reynolds' *Consumer Behaviour and Marketing Management* (Houghton Mifflin, 1967) provides a good guide to the basic sociology and psychology which underlies this subject but is not as applied as its title indicates. Robertson's *Consumer Behaviour* (Scott Foresman, 1971) is a short, rather academic text.

Texts of British origin are few and far between. *Marketing and Customer Behaviour* (Pergamon, 1972) is written by a Canadian professor (Jenkins) of business administration but is aimed at readers in the United Kingdom. Although it is not strongly grounded in the behavioural sciences, it contains useful illustrative data and makes a strong plea for consumer researchers to produce applicable results. Dawson's *The Marketing Environment* (Croom Helm, 1979) puts marketing management into the wider context of consumer behaviour, retailing systems and social change. Chisnall's *Marketing: A Behavioural Analysis* (McGraw-Hill, 1975) covers much the same ground as the present book but in a rather less critical manner.

Among books of readings, *Perspectives on Consumer Behaviour*, by Kassarjian and Robertson (Scott Foresman, 1973), stands out as a carefully selected set of articles and specially commissioned papers which offer a much-needed supplement to any textbook.

Except in the spheres of attitude measurement and change, few specialised works have appeared which link a particular area of behavioural science to consumer decision making. Zimbardo and Ebbesen's *Influencing Attitudes and Changing Behaviour* (Addison-Wesley, 1970) can still be recommended as a book written primarily for social psychologists which is nevertheless highly applicable to the marketing area, while Hughes's *Attitude Measurement for Marketing Strategies* (Scott Foresman, 1971) relates testing techniques directly to managerial concerns. Oppenheim's *Questionnaire Design and Attitude*

201

Measurement (Heinemann, 1966), which has been frequently reprinted, is also an invaluable guide to this field. *Attitudes: Selected Readings* (2nd edition, Penguin, 1973) presents a selection of journal papers which are easily assimilated by the non specialist. Another readable introduction is Reich and Adcock's *Values, Attitudes and Behaviour Change* (Methuen, 1976).

Two recent books by Mostyn can be recommended for the accurate way in which they apply psychological concepts to consumer research and marketing management: *Handbook of Motivational and Attitude Research Techniques*, and *The Attitude Behaviour Relationship* (MCB Publications, 1977-8).

General introductions to human social interaction which can be recommended to marketing students and managers are comparatively rare. Most sociologists and social psychologists have written for restricted audiences. Aronson's *The Social Animal* (2nd edition, Freeman, 1976) is an exception; it contains chapters on mass communication, propaganda and persuasion and explains these complex processes in terms which make its subject matter readily applicable to problems of consumer behaviour. The same author's *Readings About the Social Animal* (2nd edition, Freeman, 1976) contains complementary sections dealing with conformity, mass communication and persuasion, gain loss theory and group behaviour. Other introductions include Gahagan's *Interpersonal and Group Behaviour* and *Social Behaviour* by Wheldall (both Methuen, 1975). A useful source of information on the pervasiveness of class as a determinant of social behaviour is Reid's *Social Class Differences in Britain* (Open Books, 1977) which brings together statistics which are usually diversely published, many of which are directly applicable to marketing. Some of the social effects of groups, including the family and social classes, are documented in Midgley and Christopher's *Consumers in Action* (MCB, 1975) which covers the application areas of fashion trends and consumer choice, household decision making and the adoption of innovations.

Finally, in connection with the more specialised topics dealt with in the concluding chapter, Ehrenberg's *Repeat Buying* (North Holland, 1974) concerns patterns of customer loyalty; *Consumerism*, edited by Mann (MCB, 1978), and Foxall's *Consumerism: Issues, Developments and Sources of Information* (Retailing and Planning Associates, 1978) are, respectively, a useful selection of readings on the consumer protection movement and an introduction to the social and economic issues involved in consumerism. Mary Tuck's *How Do We Choose?* (Methuen, 1976) presents a clear exposition of the approach to attitude measurement pioneered by Fishbein together with an account of the inadequacies of current model-building practices in marketing education and research.

INDEX